The
Soup Sisters
Family Cookbook

The
Soup Sisters
Family Cookbook

MORE THAN 100 FAMILY-FRIENDLY RECIPES TO MAKE AND SHARE WITH KIDS OF ALL AGES

EDITED BY

SHARON HAPTON

WITH GWENDOLYN RICHARDS

appetite

by RANDOM HOUSE

Library and Archives Canada Cataloguing in Publication is available upon request.
ISBN: 978-0-14-753055-4
eBook ISBN: 978-0-14-753056-1

Cover and book design: Rachel Cooper
Cover image: Shallon Cunningham, Salt Food Photography
Photography: Julie Van Rosendaal
Photographs on page 72: Curtis Pelletier

Printed and bound in China

Published in Canada by Appetite by Random House®,
a division of Penguin Random House Canada Limited.

www.penguinrandomhouse.ca

10   9   8   7   6   5   4   3   2   1

appetite
by RANDOM HOUSE
Penguin
Random
House

contents

soup comes full circle

Welcome to our third volume of Soup Sisters recipes, yet another way to send "hugs in a bowl" out into the world. The series began in 2012 when we produced the inaugural *Soup Sisters Cookbook*, which very quickly became a bestseller. In 2014, our Broth Brothers contributed to our second edition. And, now . . . drum roll, please . . . we present our *Soup Sisters Family Cookbook*.

Featuring recipes not only from chefs, food professionals and Soup Sisters, but from more than 30 children too, this volume makes the Soup Sisters cookbook family complete. We now have a full circle of soup makers, all of whom have contributed—with love and kindness—recipes to our cookbooks.

Often proffered to friends and neighbors at a time of crisis, the message of comfort that soup carries can be as powerful as the soup itself. It is through the making and delivering of nurturing and nourishing soup to local emergency shelters that Soup Sisters has become one of Canada's premier national volunteer organizations, focused on supporting women and children escaping domestic violence.

To date, we have proudly delivered nearly 1 million "hugs in a bowl" nationwide. And, with the making and modest donation of nutritious, homemade soup, the lives of women, children and youth are made a little less isolating and lonely.

As with all of our cookbooks, this edition is a great compilation of soup recipes and soup-making stories that encompass the best of the human spirit: sharing, caring and nurturing. Above all, this book is an expression of the soup makers' core value— universal to both child and adult—of taking care of one another in a kind and simple way. It should come as no surprise that our younger generation cares deeply about their communities and peers. Kids absolutely understand what it means to comfort others with healthy and nutritious food. The pride and generosity with which they share their own soup creations with other kids is enough to make me want to take them all home with me!

Soup Sisters recognized early on that young people very much want to contribute too. As our adult programming launched and expanded, we quickly turned our attention to finding ways to serve this impressionable demographic and offer kids their own way to make a difference.

Our Summer Stock and Souper Kids programs began in 2013 and 2015 respectively, and are designed to introduce youth to the camaraderie of the kitchen while teaching cooking skills and entry-level philan- thropy. Through these programs, kids make soup for their peers who are in need. It is a personal and creative way to show their support and caring for friends they will likely never meet, but whose lives they can touch in a direct and compassionate way.

Our first kids' soup-making session took place in Calgary where Scott Riege, who was 12 years old at the time, fundraised to bring his entire class to a Soup Sisters event. His mom, who had already booked a Soup Sisters session for her friends, gave him her coveted time slot. Our veteran volunteers were a bit apprehensive about having thirty 12-year-old kids in the kitchen. Within moments of their arrival, however, we could all feel their excitement and anticipation. These incredible kids put their heart and soul into their soup making, and with great enthusiasm produced hundreds of quarts of soup that day for the Calgary Women's Emergency Shelter, so moms and kids would get to enjoy many meals of hearty and heartwarming nourishment.

As with all of our events, our youth and kids programs place great emphasis on education and awareness. Eager youngsters listen to a speaker from the recipient shelter who provides statistics on kids their own age transitioning from street culture into mainstream society and how appreciative they are to know that they are peer supported.

Their spirit and dedication inspired me to devote this cookbook to the kids who have embraced the concept of soup philanthropy with such enthusiasm. More than 30 Souper Kids from ages 5 to 17 have contributed their favorite recipes to this edition. In this book, you will find everything from homey family recipes that have been passed down from generation to generation to unique sophisticated soups created by *MasterChef Junior* contestants.

Many of these terrific young people have already made a charitable impact in their own communities and beyond. Good food, and the sharing of it, is important to them. They have set off on their own course to make the world a better place, whether they are volunteering in our regular programming, creating welcoming soup label artwork for Syrian refugees (as many elementary and junior high classes did in winter 2016 for our special Soup for Syrians event; see pages vi and 196), or looking for other ways to get involved. It gives me great pride to share some of their stories with you.

I will start with Scott Riege. With his enthusiasm and that of his classmates, the Souper Kids program was born. Scott also appears on page ii with my adorable niece, Taya.

Scott Riege, 14 years old, Calgary, Alberta
I am a Grade 9 student at Bishop Pinkham Junior High in Calgary. When I was in Grade 6 at École Holy Name, I had to compete for a ticket to We Day by telling how I wanted to make a difference in my community. I chose Soup Sisters with my friend Tobin because our moms had been to a Soup Sisters event, and I like the fact that the organization helps kids my age who are in need. You should know that we did win an opportunity to go to We Day at Calgary's Saddledome in October 2014. It was awesome.

After We Day, Tobin and I decided that we would actually deliver on the promise we made in our presentation to our school. We would host a Soup Sisters event for our whole Grade 6 class. To do that, Tobin and I needed to raise money to pay for the event. We set a goal of $1,000 to host the event and what was left over would be a donation.

To raise our money, we did bottle drives in our communities and with our hockey teams. We did odd jobs like raking leaves and shoveling snow for neighbors. Tobin made soup for family members in exchange for a donation. I made four butcher-block cutting boards and sold them for a total of $500.

On January 7, 2015, we had our Soup Sisters event at the Calgary Cookbook Co. with our class. In order to participate, we asked our classmates to make a minimum donation of $15 to Soup Sisters. It was an awesome afternoon. Sharon Hapton was there to tell us about Soup Sisters; Randy Chevrier, who was then playing for the Calgary Stampeders football team, joined us as a surprise guest. He was inspirational and told us he was impressed by our becoming leaders in our community at such a young age. We also got to try on his Grey Cup rings, which was cool. It was also really great that my aunt, a crisis counselor with the Calgary Women's Emergency Shelter, came to tell us where our soup would go and how it would help women and children in Calgary leaving a domestic abuse situation. Our class raised a total of $1,860, half of which was a donation directly to Soup Sisters.

I feel proud of what our class did on that day in January. We feel honored to have inspired Souper Kids, and Tobin and I were pretty happy to raise $800 more than our goal of $1,000. All our hard work felt like it mattered. What was also cool is we got a message from my aunt at Calgary Women's Emergency Shelter the very next day that our soup had been delivered.

What I learned from this experience was that soup is easy to make and that setting goals and working to achieve them feels good, especially when you do it with friends. I also learned that I can make a difference, even today. So can you.

Abby Major, 12 years old, *MasterChef Junior* (Season 2), Winchester, Virginia
I love to help others with my passion for food and cooking. In my hometown we have an annual Chefs' Dinner where local chefs prepare a multi-course meal as a fundraiser for our free medical clinic. I have participated in this event for the past two years. It is a lot of fun to be cooking with these talented chefs and it's all for a very good cause. I have lots of great memories about cooking, but my most vivid ones are of baking pies and bread with my grandmother. She has taught me so much!

To help out in my community, my friends and I set up lemonade stands for charity a few times a year. We love to support three in particular: SPCA, Evans Home (foster care) and Blue Ridge Wildlife Center. I would really like to make the world a better place. I like to research ways to help wildlife. In the spring of 2016, my Girls on the Run team held a supply drive to get needed supplies for the Blue Ridge Wildlife Center.

Logan Guleff, 15 years old, Winner of *MasterChef Junior* (Season 3), Memphis, Tennessee
Most people know I am a junior chef, but they don't know that I love community service almost as much as cooking. Whether I am passing out water at a race, cooking for the unsheltered or helping an animal, I know I am putting "good" into the world.

People may know I started cooking at age 2, but they don't really know that I have been working on helping my community almost as long. I first

started with participating in food drives. Then my mom let me help in a local soup kitchen at the age of 8. My friend John (one of the organizers of the kitchen staff) let me work the line at the kitchen. They feed 150 people two times a week and have been doing this for about 75 years: a mind-blowing amount of meals. I really learned to respect my own food so much more by doing this. I also cook two meals a year for Room in the Inn and have helped the local Rotary Club prepare bagged meals for Haiti. I still help with several food drives a year, and volunteer with many other charities. Since winning *MasterChef Junior*, I believe I have helped raise over $1 million in charitable giving!

My mom makes me homemade chicken soup and then uses it to cook pastina—that, to me, is my mama's love on a spoon. I always feel better when she breaks out the pastina. We get the pastina pasta from New York, so it is really special.

On one occasion, I went to the soup kitchen with the cub scouts, but the cooking was finished. I wasn't thrilled, to be honest—I wanted to work the kitchen—but I passed out Christmas gifts as I was asked to do. Then, after it was all over, an elderly African American man came in but he was too late for food. John grabbed me and we raced to the kitchen. No one is turned away. I made two microwaved frozen white bread sandwiches with pepperoni and cheese. We grabbed some leftover yogurt cups and some granola bars and John asked me to serve the gentleman.

Now, John introduced me as the "kid who shook President Obama's hand," which is true and crazy at the same time. The elderly man shook my hand, the hand that touched the president's, and he thanked me for cooking for him. He said he was honored. I cried, he cried.

I know I am truly lucky to never have felt the true sting of hunger and I am forever humbled by that man and his gratitude for a simple sandwich.

Zac Kara, 14 years old, *MasterChef Junior* (Season 4), Orlando, Florida

Everybody has to eat. It is this simple common ground that we, as a people of different colors, cultures, geographies and beliefs, all share. Like the red blood that flows in us all, food is an incredible force that unites us. It brings people together, whether it's baking cookies with your mom, having a family dinner or creating a gourmet dish. A simple tomato can end up as pasta sauce or part of a salad, stew, salsa, curry or even some soup!

Food breaks all barriers, as it is all about sharing and bringing people together. When I cook a meal for someone, the most rewarding thing that I wait and hold my breath for is a huge smile dancing on their face. It gives me a great source of happiness, and makes me want to continue cooking.

Lastly, when you cook, you can do anything that you want. Anyone can toss ingredients in many different ways and combinations. When I cook, I have no boundaries, no barriers. The result is always a plate of warmth, happiness and love.

Skylar and Chloe Sinow, 15 and 13 years old, Kids Can Cook Gourmet, Vancouver, British Columbia

Soup Sisters is an amazing organization, and we feel deeply blessed to be part of a program that is life changing for so many people. What excites us the most is the Souper Kids program. It completely fits with our passion for knowing what you are eating and creating amazing food. We truly believe that we need to get kids into the kitchen and make it a priority that they grow up surrounded by good, fair, natural foods. We want for it to be natural for kids to reach for something healthy instead of unhealthy (like processed snacks) and allow them to make these choices into their future long and happy lives.

There is no better way to teach kids about food than getting them cooking and there is no better food to start on than soup. Soup is nutritious and fun to make. As well, it is amazing that you can literally take anything in your pantry and turn it into a delicious filling meal. Soup is a great way to learn about what flavors combine well and it can be a truly creative adventure. After this is all done, you can sit down with your family and feel the joy of other people tasting and enjoying your healthy, homemade soup.

Liam Lewis, 15 years old, The Little Locavore, Vancouver, British Columbia

I can't imagine what it would be like if I didn't have the support of the food community that has embraced me, my chef friends and my family. I hope that I can use the skills I am learning to help others who are less fortunate. I have been involved for the past few years in cooking for DinnerPartyYVR, and donating all the funds from my dinners to Quest Food Exchange in Vancouver. It is a great organization that helps reduce hunger with dignity through its non-profit grocery markets.

I have huge respect for the Soup Sisters for being so caring and dedicated, so it is an honor to be contributing my recipe to this book.

These are just some of our Souper Kids. On page 198, please take a look at the biographies of all of our kid contributors. They are all beautiful, kind, bright and incredible beings. Simply experiencing their integrity is as joyful and fulfilling as a good bowl of comforting soup.

Yours in soup,

Sharon Hapton

Founder and CEO,
Soup Sisters and Broth Brothers

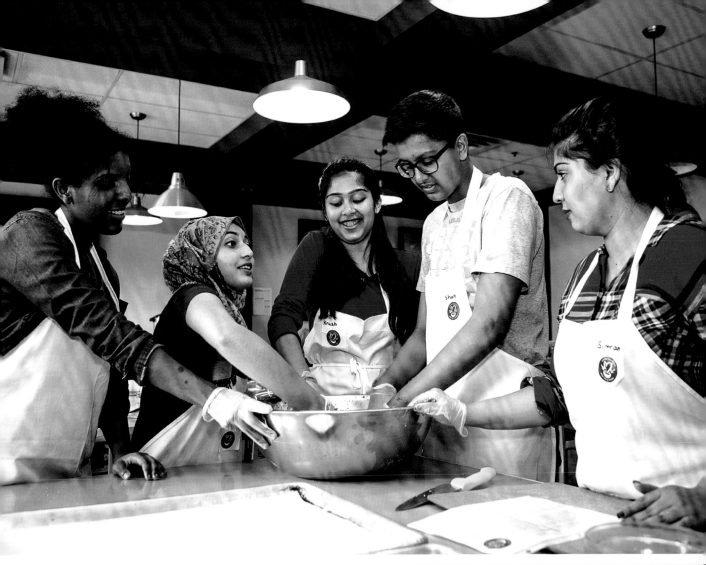

in the kitchen with kids

Making soup with kids is a great way to teach all kinds of cooking skills, as many soup recipes are easy and involve a range of basic techniques. I asked my friend Julie Van Rosendaal, who likes to say that "anything goes" with kids in the kitchen, about how kids of all ages can get involved in the cooking process. Julie is a mom, a cookbook author and a CBC radio food columnist, and she also has a fantastic blog, www.dinnerwithjulie.com. Here's what she said:

"Teaching your kids to be comfortable in the kitchen can be one of the most useful life skills you pass on to them; in fact, how you spend time in the kitchen can help establish positive feelings about cooking and mealtime preparation early on. Some of my fondest childhood memories involve dinner simmering on the stove after school (my sisters and I were in charge of planning one meal a week, and we looked forward to trying new recipes and having the authority to decide what the family would eat), all of us together at the table on a regular week-night, and baking with my grandma, even when I mostly watched.

We often don't give kids enough credit when it comes to culinary creativity. With cooking, the more you do the more you learn, and what better way to spend screen-free time together? Following recipes is a great way for kids to learn the basics of reading and math while developing cooking skills that are essential for their long-term health—physical and financial—and that of their future families. Getting your kids involved with their food will encourage them to try new things and lay the groundwork for a healthy lifestyle. Besides, kids take pride in what they create and are much more likely to actually *eat* something they've proudly prepared themselves. Although most parents think of cookies, muffins and pizza as designated "kid food," what they choose to make may surprise you. A pot of soup is a perfect starting point: tossing ingredients into a pot and simmering it until it's done is an easy concept for kids to grasp, and there are plenty of opportunities to get creative with seasonings, as well as veggies to chop, stock to pour and stirring to do. Best of all, for the most part measurements are pretty lax—unlike baking, you have some wiggle room when you make a pot of soup.

The experience can begin before you reach the kitchen. When shopping, ask your kids for help selecting produce by squeezing and sniffing fruits and vegetables, and try to choose something they've never eaten before. Introduce them to different varieties of foods by exploring your nearest Chinatown or Italian market. Next time you're at the library, stroll through the cookbook section and let the kids choose some new ones to take home. And in the kitchen, explain where each ingredient comes from, who grows or raises it, and what makes it good (or not so good) for us.

Kids are inherently creative and very hands-on, and the kitchen is a great place to explore their heightened senses—smell, touch, sight, sound and, of course, taste. Most kids wind up making a mess, so try to remember that it's all a learning experience."

I hope Julie's words will encourage and inspire you to bring your kids into the kitchen with you! You can read her safety tips for cooking with kids on page 14, and her recipe on page 45, too!

getting started

No matter the style of soup, the basic building blocks are all the same. With a well-stocked kitchen—from pantry to fridge—putting together a hearty and comforting pot of soothing soup is a snap.

Here's what we recommend having on hand so soup can always be on the menu.

the pantry

From pulses and pastas to spices and stocks, most of the soup-making ingredients are going to be found in the pantry cupboard.

beans, lentils and other pulses

Whether dried or canned, beans add lots of heartiness to soups. Having canned beans in the cupboard makes it much simpler and faster to throw together a pot of soup, but we like to have dried beans in the cupboard too. They're less expensive and just need a little overnight soak or precook to get them soup ready.

To prepare dry beans, first pick over the beans to look for any grit or anything else that doesn't belong, then rinse and drain them. Put the beans in a large saucepan and add enough water so they're covered by 1 inch. Cover it all up with a lid and let the beans soak overnight. Drain well before using in the recipe.

To precook beans, follow the same instructions, but instead of letting them sit overnight, simply bring them to a boil over high heat and let them cook for 2 minutes. Remove the saucepan from the heat, cover and let stand for 1 hour before continuing with the soup recipe.

Dried lentils and split peas, on the other hand, don't need any preparation before adding them to

soups. They cook quickly and thicken up soups nicely, so are great to have around.

dried herbs and spices

Fresh herbs have the most flavor, but are not always something we have on hand. In a pinch, dried herbs work well too. And spices transform a standard soup into something special. Having these dried herbs and spices will allow you to make any of the soups in this cookbook:

- Basil
- Bay leaves
- Cayenne
- Celery salt
- Chili powder
- Cinnamon, ground and sticks
- Cloves, ground and whole
- Coriander, ground and seeds
- Cumin, ground and seeds
- Curry powder
- Fennel seed, ground
- Garam masala
- Garlic powder
- Ginger, ground
- Italian herb seasoning
- Marjoram leaves
- Nutmeg, ground
- Onion powder
- Oregano, ground and leaves
- Paprika, regular and smoked
- Parsley
- Peppercorns
  - black
  - Sichuan
  - white
- Red chili flakes
- Rosemary, ground and leaves
- Saffron threads
- Sage, ground
- Star anise, ground and whole
- Sumac
- Tarragon
- Thyme
- Turmeric, ground

oils

Canola, grapeseed, sunflower, vegetable or regular olive oils are all excellent for sautéing vegetables as a base for soups or frying other ingredients to be added in. Save the expensive, fruity or grassy extra virgin olive oil for drizzling over top or serving alongside with some nice bread and maybe a splash of balsamic vinegar.

rice and pasta

Different types of rice are great to add to soups to thicken them up or add heartiness. Rice can also be used to replace noodles in certain soups for something a little different. Soups are an excellent way to use up all those random bits of pasta left in the cupboard too. Throw some handfuls of macaroni into a minestrone or send secret messages by using alphabet-shaped pasta in place of standard spaghetti noodles.

salt and pepper

All soups benefit from proper seasoning. Unless the recipe states otherwise, we use kosher salt and freshly ground black pepper when making soups in this book.

When it comes to adding salt, it's easy to add more but impossible to take it out, so season gently as you go, and then check the taste just before serving, adding more if needed.

Add a little salt at a time, stirring it in completely before tasting it, and then repeat until the soup tastes just right, with all the flavors popping perfectly.

Fancy salts in different colors, textures and flavors are a fun and interesting way to garnish your soup, adding a little something special at the very end. Just remember that they will add more salt to the soup so under-season slightly before sprinkling the fancy salt over the top.

Freshly ground pepper has more flavor than the regular stuff from the spice rack, so a little goes a long way. Hold back a bit to garnish on the soup at the end or serve up soup with the pepper grinder on the table so everyone can add how much they'd like.

stock

Having homemade stock in the freezer is ideal, but in a pinch store-bought cartons can save on time. We prefer organic varieties in our cupboards. Just keep in mind that ready-made stocks or stock cubes do contain higher levels of sodium, so watch how much salt you add to the soup if that's what you use.

Looking to make your own? Head to page 15 for our easy recipes.

the vegetable patch

Onions, celery and carrots are the secret stars of many soups, so you'll always want to have them on hand. They all keep for a long time—celery and carrots in the crisper and onions in a cool, dark, dry spot—and even when they start to look a bit limp, they'll be perfect for adding to a pot of stock.

Potatoes, root vegetables and squash, when hidden away in a cool, dry cupboard, will also be ready to go for long periods of time, so stock up for times of soup cravings.

Garlic adds lots of flavor, so it's a must-have. Don't worry if it starts to sprout green shoots out of the top of the bulbs; those can be thrown into stock too.

the fridge and freezer

bacon

Few ingredients can add the same flavor as bacon. Salty and meaty, it elevates even the simplest soup. Fry it up at the start of soup making and cook your vegetables in the rendered fat (instead of butter or oil), top soups with crunchy cooked bits or even add some to the pot when making homemade stock.

Feel free to also experiment with pancetta, bacon's Italian cousin, which is cured but not smoked.

butter

Nothing is better than butter. To control the salt best, use unsalted, then season the soup later. But we like salted butter on toast or bread served alongside a big bowl of soup. If that's all you have, use that and simply ease up on the amount of salt you add to the soup.

cream

Creamy soups are just that because of the addition of silky, rich cream. Milk just doesn't give that same smooth flavor. A little goes a long way, though, so don't worry too much about the higher fat content.

herbs

There is no substitute for fresh herbs. Their clean flavor and bright greenness add nice pops of color and brighten up the taste of soup in a way that dried herbs just can't match. Stirring them into soups at the last minute keeps them at their best and brightest.

If you have a green thumb, herbs fresh from your own garden are excellent. But parsley, cilantro, basil, mint and more are also readily available at most grocery stores and will stay fresh for a few weeks in the fridge when stored properly.

First, rinse the bunches of herbs thoroughly and then let them dry for a few minutes. Fill clean glasses or glass jam jars about halfway with water and then place the herb bunches in them like a bouquet, stems under water. Cover with a plastic bag—like the produce ones from the grocery store—squeeze out the extra air and then secure the bag around the glass or jar with an elastic band. Store in the fridge. Whenever you need some fresh herbs, just unwrap, snip or tear off what you need and then cover them back up again.

lemons and limes

Citrus adds lots of bright, sunny flavor and there is no replacement for the real thing. Look for lemons and limes that are firm, are heavy for their size and have smooth, colorful skin; they should smell good when given a sniff.

Keep them in the crisper. Lemons will last longer than limes and can sit on the counter for about a week before they should head to the fridge, where they will last for a couple more weeks. Limes should be refrigerated after a day or two, and then they will last just as long as lemons.

If recipes call for zest and juice, be sure to zest first. It's too tricky to do it the other way around.

stock

After making a big batch of homemade stock (see pages 15 to 17), package some of it up and store it in the freezer for future soup cravings. For tips on how to freeze soup and stock safely, turn to page 17.

essential equipment

blender

Making soup super smooth is a cinch with a blender. You can either use one that sits on the countertop or an immersion blender that purées the soup right in the pot.

A countertop blender is the kind with a goblet that sits on a motorized base. It can make soups silky smooth, but there is a trick to keeping soup from splattering all over the kitchen walls. For hot liquids, these steps are best done with adult supervision.

1. Remove the center cap from the blender lid, so steam can escape. Then, fill the blender only

about halfway with equal parts of soup chunks and liquid. Put the lid back and place a folded dry dishcloth over the hole where the cap was to keep all the soup inside. It's safe to place your hand over the cloth to hold the lid in place while the blender is doing its work.

2. Start it on low and slowly bring it up to full speed, blending until the soup is super smooth. Pour that into a clean pot and continue blending the soup in small batches until it's all puréed.

Immersion blenders—also known as hand or wand blenders—can go right into the soup pot to purée the soup on the spot. It takes a bit longer to make the soup smooth, but they are fun to swirl through the soup and are much easier to clean. This is the method we prefer in this book, as it is safer for kids—just be careful not to splash the hot soup!

1. Place the end of the immersion blender in the soup, right down at the bottom of the pot, and then turn it on.
2. Move it around the bottom of the pot to keep the soup from splattering and keep blending until it's all smooth.

cheesecloth

Cheesecloth is handy for tying up little bouquet garni bundles and for straining stock to keep all the bits and pieces of bone, vegetables and spices out. Just use some of the cloth to line a sieve before straining to remove any impurities for perfect homemade stock.

cutting boards

Wood or plastic cutting boards are the best for chopping all your soup ingredients because marble, glass or hard composite boards will dull your knives.

knives

Sharp knives are a soup maker's best tool. While dull ones are dangerous because they slip and don't go where they're told to, a sharp knife goes exactly to the place that needs to be chopped or sliced, and that will ensure nice, uniformly cut ingredients that will also cook evenly.

pots

Stainless steel pots and saucepans with heavy bottoms make the best soups. The thicker the bottom of the pot, the better it will conduct heat, making it easier to keep vegetables from getting burnt or soup boiling too vigorously.

Having a variety of pots in different sizes is helpful, so you have just the right one for making big batches of stock or reheating a little soup for lunch or dinner.

sieve

A large, fine-mesh sieve is great for straining impurities out of stock (add a cheesecloth liner, if you wish, to catch every little bit) and for making sure puréed soups are as smooth as can be. Coarse- or fine-mesh sieves can be used to capture any lumps after puréeing a soup.

vegetable peelers

There are lots of shapes and sizes when it comes to vegetable peelers. The fastest and most efficient is the Y-shaped or speed peeler, but the most important thing is to get one with a good grip that feels good in your hand.

slicing, chopping, peeling and prepping

All good soup recipes start with some prep—getting veggies and other ingredients ready for the pot, so by the time you're cooking, everything is ready to go.

The trick for having everything cooked at the same time is to have evenly sized ingredients. If all the chunks of an ingredient are the same size when they go into the pot, they'll all be ready at the same time. Here's how to prep some common vegetables:

to chop an onion

1. Slice the top off the onion and then just barely shave off the straggly root end. (Keeping most of the root will help hold the onion together while chopping.)
2. Cut the onion in half, from the root end to the top.
3. Peel off the skin and lay the onion halves on their flat sides.
4. Make lengthwise cuts, about two-thirds of the way toward the root end.
5. Slice the onion crosswise to chop it. For a finely chopped onion, make the cuts closer together.

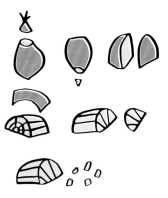

to chop herbs

1. For herbs with a tough or woody stem, like thyme or rosemary, pull the leaves off and discard the stems. For herbs with soft stems, like cilantro or parsley, just chop off the thicker stems and discard them.
2. Pile all the leaves together and chop a few times in one direction for coarsely chopped herbs or continue chopping for those that need to be finely chopped.

to prepare garlic

1. Place the flat side of your knife on an unpeeled clove of garlic and press down with your palm to crush it. Peel off the skin.

2. To slice it, use a sharp knife to make thin strips of garlic. To finely chop, use a sharp knife and keep the point of the blade against the cutting board while moving the knife up and down from side to side until the garlic is in tiny pieces. To mince, keep chopping the garlic and then use the flat side of the knife to crush the pieces into a purée.

A rasp grater can also be used to mince garlic to a purée.

to mince ginger

1. Using the tip of a regular spoon, peel off the thin outer layer of the ginger. (This is a great task for kids!)

2. Using a rasp grater, grate the ginger into a fine pulp, or very finely chop it with a knife.

Any unused ginger can be wrapped in aluminum foil and kept in the freezer.

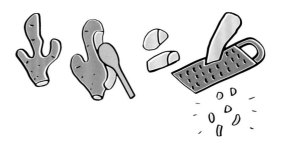

a key to the icons

Vegetarian soups might include eggs and/or dairy products, so check the recipe carefully if these are foods you'd rather live without. Some of the recipes marked with this icon can be made vegetarian if you choose to use vegetable stock.

Vegan soups are derived from vegetables or grains; they are free of all dairy products and eggs (although some soups might call for optional non-vegan garnishes). Vegan soups are also suitable for vegetarians.

Gluten-free soups contain no flour products, whole grains or bread. Some may contain items, such as soy sauce or stock, or suggest garnishes that are available in gluten-free formats so be sure to read the ingredients on the jar, bottle or package before you buy.

A **wooden spoon** indicates a helpful hint or tip that gives you a little more detail about the recipe; for example, a serving suggestion or information on alternative ingredients.

A **soup bowl** highlights a story, tip or tale that comes directly from the chef, food professional, Soup Sister or Souper Kid who contributed the recipe.

a word about kitchen safety

Kitchen safety is subjective—there isn't one age at which kids are able to handle knives or hot elements; it has more to do with their skill and confidence level. When kids are in the kitchen, make sure you're close at hand—younger kids will likely need help at the stove—and always ensure hot pots are not within reach of curious types who may pull them over on themselves.

When starting out with knife skills, offer them a plastic knife or metal butter knife if it makes you more comfortable, and stay close by; soft veggies like mushrooms and zucchini are easy to cut (if they roll around, cut them in half to stabilize them). If they go to town and chop more vegetables than they need, just freeze the extras—they'll be perfect for tossing into your next pot of soup.

If you have young or inexperienced children, there are plenty of tasks kids of all ages can take on that don't require knives or heat. They might like to stir, roll, bash, shake, pour, knead, measure or spread ingredients.

stocking up

The secret to making the best homemade soups is starting with the best home-made stock. There is something so comforting about simmering a pot of it on the stove and it doesn't take much effort to transform a few ingredients into a tasty base for future soup cravings. Make a large batch, then store it in your freezer so you're always ready to simmer up some soup from scratch at any time. Here's how to make, then chill and safely store, your homemade stock:

chicken, turkey or beef stock

You can use raw chicken or turkey bones—from chicken portions you've deboned—or cooked ones from a Sunday roast. Buy meaty beef bones (preferably those with some marrow in them) from your butcher for the beef version of this recipe.

Makes about 24 cups

24 cups cold water (approx.)
5 lb chicken or turkey bones or 8 lb beef
   bones
1 carrot, peeled and finely chopped
1 onion, finely chopped
1 stalk celery, finely chopped

2 cloves garlic
3 sprigs parsley
2 bay leaves
1 sprig thyme
10 whole black peppercorns
2 whole cloves

1. Combine all the ingredients in a large pot. The water should cover everything. If it doesn't, add more water until all the ingredients are submerged.

2. Bring to a boil, uncovered, over high heat. As soon as bubbles start to break the surface, reduce the heat to a bare simmer.

3. Simmer, uncovered, for 2 hours, never letting the stock boil. (Boiling results in a cloudy stock but, if that happens, it's still completely edible and tasty; it's just not as pretty as a clear stock.)

4. While the stock simmers gently, use a large metal spoon to occasionally skim off any impurities that float to the surface.

5. Line a fine-mesh sieve with a double layer of cheesecloth. Ladle the stock and solids through the sieve set over a large bowl or clean pot. Discard the solids and use the stock immediately, or freeze in small containers for future use. (See page 17 for how to safely chill stock.)

fish stock

While chicken, beef and vegetable stock can all be made ahead and frozen for when the urge to make soup strikes, fish stock should be made fresh and used right away. The good news is it takes far less time than its meaty cousins.

If you don't have fish bones and heads on hand—and, really, who does?—buy them from your fish store. But avoid those from oily fish like salmon and mackerel as they will make your stock cloudy.

Makes about 24 cups

24 cups cold water (approx.)
5 lb fish bones or fresh fish heads (gills
    removed)
1 carrot, peeled and finely chopped
1 onion, finely chopped
1 stalk celery, finely chopped

2 cloves garlic
3 sprigs parsley
2 bay leaves
1 sprig fresh thyme
10 whole black peppercorns

1. Combine all the ingredients in a large pot. The water should cover everything. If it doesn't, add more water until all the ingredients are submerged.

2. Bring to a boil, uncovered, over high heat. As soon as bubbles start to break the surface, reduce the heat to a bare simmer.

3. Simmer, uncovered, for 20 to 30 minutes, never letting the stock boil. (Boiling results in a cloudy stock but, if that happens, it's still completely edible and tasty; it's just not as pretty as a clear stock.)

4. While the stock simmers gently, use a large metal spoon to occasionally skim off any impurities that float to the surface.

5. Line a fine-mesh sieve with a double layer of cheesecloth. Ladle the stock and solids through the sieve set over a large bowl or clean pot. Discard the solids and use the stock immediately.

vegetable stock

Vegetable stocks are great to have because they make serving up a vegetarian or vegan soup a snap. The stock's light flavor also won't overwhelm other ingredients in the soup.

Makes about 24 cups

24 cups cold water (approx.)
2 carrots, peeled and finely chopped
2 onions, finely chopped
2 stalks celery, finely chopped
2 cloves garlic

3 sprigs parsley
2 bay leaves
1 sprig fresh thyme
10 whole black peppercorns

1. Combine all the ingredients in a large pot. The water should cover everything. If it doesn't, add more water until all the ingredients are submerged.

2. Bring to a boil, uncovered, over high heat. Once it's boiling, reduce the heat to medium.

3. Boil gently for 1 hour, never letting the stock boil vigorously. (Unlike meat and fish stocks, you can still boil vegetable stock quite rapidly because there are no proteins to make the stock cloudy. So, you'll be done much more quickly.)

4. Strain the stock by ladling it through a fine-mesh sieve set over a large bowl or clean pot. Discard the solids and use the stock immediately, or freeze it in small containers for future use. (See below for how to safely chill stock.)

chilling and storing soup and stock

Once you've made a batch of stock or soup, it's important to know how to properly chill it before putting it in the fridge or freezer.

1. Put the plug in a clean kitchen sink. Place your pot of hot soup or stock in the sink and add ice so it comes one-quarter of the way up the side of the pot. (If it's winter, you can use freshly fallen snow instead of ice.)

2. Fill the sink with cold water from the tap until it reaches the same level as the soup in the pot. Keep stirring the soup until it cools down to lukewarm or body temperature.

3. Transfer the soup to smaller containers and store them in the fridge or freezer.

garden grown

FROM THE MOMENT THE FIRST TINY GREEN SHOOTS SPRING UP through the soil, to the days when the leaves begin to turn golden and it's time to pick the last of the bounty, a garden can provide an abundance of tasty soup ingredients. In this chapter, you'll find soups for all seasons where fresh vegetables take a starring role. Tomatoes that slowly ripen on their bright green vines, carrots that burrow into the earth as they grow, big heads of white cauliflower nestled in a blanket of green leaves—all of these and many more make their way into some of our favorite soups.

Creamy and Bacony Asparagus Soup with Dill Croutons (page 80)

summery stew with pesto

Amanda Cohen
Chef and Owner of Dirt Candy, New York City, NY

Stew in the summer is kind of counter-intuitive but this is a really light one, which may sound impossible, but it can be done.

Makes about 4 servings

If you omit the pesto, this stew is suitable for vegans.

stew
¼ cup olive oil
1 cup finely chopped red onion
3 Tbsp minced garlic
1 Tbsp finely chopped fresh oregano or
    1 tsp dried oregano leaves (optional)
¼ tsp red chili flakes (optional)
1½ cups water or vegetable stock
1 cup finely chopped peeled potato
3 cups finely chopped zucchini
2 cups finely chopped peeled yellow
    squash

1 cup corn kernels
1 cup finely chopped roasted sweet red
    pepper (see page 115)
4 cups cored and finely chopped
    tomatoes
1 Tbsp salt
½ tsp black pepper

pesto
2 cups packed basil leaves
¼ cup freshly grated Parmesan cheese
1 Tbsp olive oil

1. For the stew, heat the olive oil in a medium pot over medium heat. Add the onion, then cook, stirring occasionally, until it is totally translucent, for about 5 minutes. Add the garlic and cook, stirring occasionally, for 4 minutes. Stir in the oregano and red chili flakes (if using).

2. Add the water and potato and bring to a boil over medium-high heat. Reduce the heat to medium-low and simmer, uncovered and stirring occasionally, until the potatoes are almost fully cooked, for about 20 minutes. Add the zucchini, yellow squash, corn and red pepper (with its juices). Simmer, stirring occasionally, for about 3 minutes.

3. Add the tomatoes, salt and pepper and bring to a simmer. Simmer, uncovered and stirring occasionally, for about 5 minutes.

4. Meanwhile, for the pesto, pulse the basil leaves, Parmesan and olive oil in a food processor until a thick paste forms.

5. To serve the stew, ladle it into warm bowls and top each serving with a generous dollop of the pesto.

easy creamy tomato soup

Anthony Rose
Chef and Owner of Bar Begonia and five other restaurants, Toronto, ON

As a kid I was a very finicky eater and could not cook for myself at all. My go-to was canned condensed tomato soup and grilled cheese. I ate this every day and my mom was quite fed up with making it for me. One day, home sick and fending for myself, I was mortified to find we had no canned tomato soup in the house! What's a kid to do? I checked through my mom's cookbooks, found a super-simple recipe, stumbled my way through it and here I am today: chef extraordinaire!

Makes about 12 servings

½ onion, chopped
5 cloves garlic
3 bay leaves, tied in a square of cheesecloth
7 leaves fresh sage
3 lb Roma tomatoes, cored and cut in half lengthwise
4½ cups whipping cream (35% MF)
¼ cup white wine
7 dashes hot pepper sauce
Salt and pepper to taste

1. In a large pot cook the onion, garlic, bay leaves and sage over low heat, stirring often, until the onion starts to soften, about 10 minutes.

2. Add the tomatoes and increase the heat to medium. Cook, uncovered and stirring occasionally, until the tomatoes are tender and have completely broken up, about 1 hour.

3. Add the cream and bring the soup to a simmer.

4. Fish out and discard the bay leaves and sage. Add the white wine and hot pepper sauce.

5. Remove the pot from the heat. Using an immersion blender in the pot, blend the soup until smooth. If you don't have an immersion blender, you can use a food processor.

6. Season the soup with salt and pepper to taste, then ladle into warm bowls. Serve with grilled cheese, of course!

maple-roasted squash and apple soup

David Robertson
Owner of The Dirty Apron Cooking School & Delicatessen, Vancouver, BC

Sweet-tart apple combines with mild butternut squash and a hint of maple syrup in this creamy fall soup.

Makes about 2 servings

10 oz butternut squash, peeled, seeded and coarsely chopped
2½ Tbsp maple syrup
1 Tbsp olive oil
1 large shallot, coarsely chopped
2 cloves garlic, minced
1 Granny Smith apple, peeled, cored and chopped
6½ Tbsp apple juice
3 Tbsp white wine
1½ cups vegetable stock
6½ Tbsp whipping cream (35% MF)
Juice of ½ a lemon
Salt and white pepper to taste

There are many great ways to garnish this soup: try thin slices of fresh apple with yogurt drizzled on top, or dollops of lightly whipped cream sprinkled with cinnamon and chives.

1. Preheat the oven to 450°F. On a large rimmed baking sheet, toss the squash with the maple syrup until the squash is well covered. Spread the squash out on the baking sheet, then roast until it browns slightly, about 15 minutes. Remove from the oven and set aside.

2. In a medium saucepan over medium heat, heat the olive oil. Add the shallot and garlic and cook, stirring, for 2 minutes. Add the apple, apple juice and white wine, then let it bubble until the liquid has reduced by half.

3. Pour in the vegetable stock and bring the soup to a boil over medium-high heat. Add the roasted squash to the pot, making sure to scrape all the pieces and juices in. Add the cream, reduce the heat to medium-low and simmer, uncovered, for about 5 minutes.

4. Remove the pot from the heat. Using an immersion blender in the pot, blend the soup until smooth. Stir in the lemon juice and season with salt and pepper to taste.

"dirty" carrot soup

Becky Hood

Chopped Canada Contestant, Soup Sister, and Chef at 39 Carden Street, Guelph, ON

Growing up on a small, rural farm, I always had access to fresh fruit and vegetables. My grandma would take me into the garden and pull things off the plants, bushes and trees. My favorites to snack on were the carrots . . . right out of the dirt! Now that I'm a professional chef, people will ask me "What is your favorite food?" and to this day, I always say "a dirty carrot." The flavor reminds me of one of the people I love most, my grandma. This recipe is dedicated to her.

Makes about 8 servings

Kids can help by doing the peeling and measuring but leave the chopping and blending to a grown-up!

"dirt"
1 Tbsp salted butter
1 cup walnuts, chopped
½ cup packed brown sugar
1 tsp ground cinnamon
Pinch of salt

soup
1 cup salted butter
1 onion, finely chopped

8 cloves garlic, minced
1 tsp finely chopped fresh thyme leaves
8 cups water or vegetable stock
8 carrots, peeled and finely chopped
1 cup orange juice
½ cup packed brown sugar
½ tsp ground nutmeg
½ tsp ground cinnamon
½ cup whipping cream (35% MF)
Salt to taste

1. For the "dirt," melt the butter in a small saucepan over medium heat. Add the walnuts and cook, stirring often, until they are evenly toasted, for about 3 minutes.

2. Add the sugar, cinnamon and salt and stir until the nuts are evenly coated. Spread the nuts out on a small baking sheet and set aside to cool completely.

3. For the soup, melt the butter in a large pot over medium heat. Add the onion and cook, stirring often, until the onion is translucent, about 7 minutes. Add the garlic and thyme, then cook, stirring, for 1 minute.

4. Add the water, carrots, orange juice, sugar, nutmeg and cinnamon. Bring to a boil over medium-high heat, then reduce the heat to medium-low and let it all simmer, uncovered, until the carrots are completely soft, about 20 minutes.

5. Remove the pot from the heat. Using an immersion blender in the pot, blend the soup until smooth, gradually adding the whipping cream as you blend.

6. Season with salt to taste. Ladle the soup into warm bowls, sprinkle each serving with the desired amount of "dirt" and enjoy!

ruby red tomato and roasted red pepper soup

Melanie Hennessey
Soup Sister

When I was a child, I found my nana made the best food. I always remember having family meals around the table daily, and that tradition was passed down to my mum. My nana's recipe became my mum's and now has been passed down to me. It's very simple, but the best. My kids love this dish almost as much as I did.

Makes about 12 servings

1 lb Roma tomatoes, cored and cut in half lengthwise

1 red onion, coarsely chopped

3 cloves garlic, peeled but left whole

1 sprig fresh thyme

Olive oil cooking spray

Salt to taste

10 cups water

2 cans (each 28 oz) diced tomatoes

2 cans (each 28 oz) roasted red peppers, drained

2 Tbsp liquid vegetable seasoning (see sidebar)

2 Tbsp packed fresh basil leaves

Pepper to taste

2 Tbsp granulated sugar

½ cup balsamic vinegar

Liquid vegetable seasoning is a soy- or wheat-based seasoning used to add meaty flavor to soups and stews. Look for it near the herbs and spices in your supermarket.

For a gluten-free soup, choose a soy-based product.

1. Preheat the oven to 350°F. Arrange the tomatoes cut side down and in a single layer on a large rimmed baking sheet. Scatter the onion, garlic and thyme evenly over the tomatoes. Spray the vegetables with olive oil to coat, then season with salt to taste. Roast until the tomatoes are well blistered and slightly browned, about 25 minutes. Discard the thyme sprig.

2. Tip the tomato mixture into a large pot. Add the water, canned tomatoes (with their juices) and roasted red peppers and liquid vegetable seasoning. Bring to a boil over medium-high heat, stirring often. Reduce the heat to medium-low, then simmer, uncovered, for 30 minutes.

3. Add the basil and season with more salt and pepper to taste. Continue simmering, uncovered, for another 20 minutes.

4. Meanwhile, make a balsamic vinegar reduction by combining the sugar and vinegar in a small saucepan. Bring to a boil over medium-high heat. Boil, stirring often, until the mixture has reduced by one third, about 3 to 5 minutes. Remove the saucepan from the heat and set aside.

5. Remove the soup pot from the heat. Using an immersion blender in the pot, blend the soup until smooth. Stir in the balsamic vinegar reduction, then season the soup with salt and pepper to taste. Ladle into warm bowls and serve.

jane morris's potato soup

Elizabeth Baird
Cookbook Author and Recipient of the Order of Canada

More than a century ago, in my grandmother Jane Morris's farm kitchen near Stratford, Ontario, she presided over a table set for 10—eight of them hungry kids. No matter how busy she was or how low supplies were, my grandmother could always rustle up a supper to nourish and please her family. In a pinch, she would make this simple potato soup—really a potato chowder—with potatoes and onions from her garden or root cellar and cream and butter from the herd of Holsteins milked morning and night. I like to think she made a big pan of biscuits to go along with the soup, and put out a hunk of cheddar made from their own milk in the nearby farmers' cooperative cheese factory.

The recipe passed on to my mother, who set her table for just four, and we loved the soup steaming hot on a winter night. I think she served it with grilled cheese sandwiches, but I may be remembering the grilled cheese only because it goes so well with soup.

Makes about 4 servings

If you like your soup a little runnier, add more stock, milk or cream. For a lighter soup, use 1% milk instead of whole milk or cream.

2 Tbsp butter
4 medium potatoes, peeled and chopped
2 small onions, chopped
2 cups chicken or vegetable stock
¼ tsp pepper
Salt to taste
2 cups whole milk (3.25% MF) or light cream (5% MF)
½ cup lightly packed parsley leaves

1. Put the butter in a large pot and set it over the lowest heat to let the butter melt. Add the potatoes and onions and stir to coat them with the butter. Cover the pot and let the vegetables cook for 5 minutes. Uncover and stir. Cover again and cook the vegetables until the onions are transparent, about 5 minutes longer.

2. Add the stock, the pepper and a little salt. Increase the heat to medium and bring to a boil. Give the potato mixture a good stir, then cover the pot and reduce the heat to low. Simmer gently until the potatoes are tender when you press them with a fork, about 15 minutes.

Awesome Add-Ins

- Peel and slice a carrot to cook with the potatoes and onions.
- Before you add the milk, stir in 1 cup of frozen peas or edamame, fresh or frozen corn kernels, shredded spinach or kale, or small or thinly sliced broccoli florets.
- Before you add the parsley, stir in 1 Tbsp snipped fresh dill, basil, chives or green onion tops.

Go-To Garnishes

- Sprinkle crushed crackers, pita or bagel crisps, melba toast, chips, croutons, or pretzel sticks over each bowl of soup.
- Garnish each bowl with shredded cheddar or havarti or grated Parmesan cheese.
- Swirl a spoonful of sour cream, plain yogurt or pesto into each bowl of soup.
- Dollop a small spoonful of herbed cream cheese into the soup just before serving and let it melt.

3. Pour in the milk and stir well. Bring the soup back to a simmer, then carefully taste your soup. If it needs more salt and pepper, now's the time to stir it in, a little at a time.

4. If you want a thicker soup with some chunks, use a potato masher or fork to mash some of the vegetables to thicken the soup. For a velvety smooth soup, use an immersion blender in the pot to blend the soup until smooth.

5. Use kitchen scissors to snip the parsley into small pieces. Stir the parsley into the soup.

6. Ladle the soup into warm bowls, and be proud of the pleasure you get from making such a pure and simple soup for your family, friends and yourself.

mexican creamy corn soup

Martha Hernandez
Soup Sister

This hearty soup is easy to prepare and perfect for lunch or dinner. Since moving to Calgary from Mexico City, we've found the flavor of sweet Alberta corn tastes just like home.

You can dress up this soup in lots of different ways! Add your favorite spices and/or fresh herbs; make it spicy by adding finely chopped jalapeños or canned chipotles in adobo sauce along with the garlic; garnish each bowl with fried tortilla strips, crumbled *queso fresco* (available at Latino grocery stores) or feta.

Makes about 4 servings

1 Tbsp canola oil or butter
½ onion, finely chopped
2 cloves garlic, minced
3 cups fresh or frozen corn kernels (see sidebar)
4 cups chicken or vegetable stock or water
1 can (12 oz) evaporated milk
Salt and pepper to taste

1. In a medium pot, heat the oil over medium heat. Add the onion and cook, stirring often, until it starts to soften, about 5 minutes. Add the garlic and cook, stirring, until it smells good, about 20 seconds.

2. Add the corn kernels and cook, stirring often, until the kernels look slightly golden brown, about 2 minutes. Scoop about two-thirds of the corn mixture from the pot and set aside for later.

3. Add the stock to the pot and bring to a boil over medium-high heat. Reduce the heat to medium-low and simmer, uncovered, for about 5 minutes.

4. Remove the pot from the heat and add the evaporated milk. Using an immersion blender in the pot, blend the soup until smooth.

5. Add the reserved corn kernel mixture back to the pot. Reheat the soup gently over medium heat and season with salt and pepper to taste. Ladle the soup into warm bowls and enjoy.

Four large ears of corn will yield 3 cups of kernels. Simply husk the ears then, working with one at a time, stand an ear on its stem end on a rimmed baking sheet and run a sturdy chef knife down the ear to slice off the kernels.

If you use water instead of chicken stock and omit the evaporated milk, this soup is suitable for vegans.

every bunny loves carrot soup

Skylar and Chloe Sinow
Ages 15 and 13, *Chopped Canada Teen Tournament*, kidscancookgourmet.com, Vancouver, BC

This soup is super healthy and delicious and the recipe is really easy to follow. Our friends helped test this recipe and they loved it.

Makes about 4 servings

2 lb carrots, peeled and chopped	Salt to taste
4 Tbsp olive oil	Maple-Candied Hazelnuts (see below)
5 to 6 cups vegetable stock	Extra virgin olive oil for drizzling
4 Tbsp maple syrup	(optional)

1. Preheat the oven to 350°F. In a large roasting pan, toss together the carrots and olive oil. Roast the carrots, uncovered and stirring every 15 minutes or so, until they are very tender, 30 to 45 minutes. If the carrots become dry while they're roasting, add a little water, 1 Tbsp at a time, to moisten them.

2. Remove the carrots from the oven and let them cool slightly. Tip the carrots into a large pot and add the stock, maple syrup and salt to taste.

3. Using an immersion blender in the pot, blend the soup until smooth with no chunks. (If there are chunks remaining, simply keep blending until smooth.)

4. Bring the soup to a simmer over medium heat, then simmer for about 45 minutes, uncovered and stirring occasionally, so the flavor develops.

5. Ladle the soup into warm bowls and add three or four maple-candied hazelnuts and a drizzle of extra virgin olive oil (if using) to each serving.

This naturally creamy soup is packed with vitamins A and C.

maple-candied hazelnuts

4 tsp maple syrup
12 to 16 hazelnuts

1. In a small saucepan over medium heat, heat the maple syrup until foamy. Add the hazelnuts and stir to combine.

2. Tip the nuts out onto a piece of parchment paper, then spread them out and make sure that none of the nuts are touching. Let cool completely.

grilled tomato and coconut soup

Jonah Joffe
Sous Chef, Alloy, Calgary, AB

Grilling vegetables caramelizes their natural sugars and makes them sweet and smoky. Here, grilled tomatoes and onions add rich flavor to a soup that has a way of satisfying my soul, no matter what the season.

Makes about 4 servings

3 lb vine-ripened tomatoes, cored and cut in half
1 large red onion, cut into rings
4 Tbsp olive oil
6 cloves garlic, coarsely chopped
2 cups canned coconut milk
1½ cups water

2 sprigs basil
3 Tbsp granulated sugar
1 tsp salt
Pepper to taste
Crumbled feta for garnish
Finely chopped cilantro for garnish
Avocado oil for drizzling

Garnishing the soup with crumbled feta adds a nice touch of saltiness without having to overseason your soup.

1. Preheat the barbecue to high (about 400°F). Grease the grill, then arrange the tomatoes, cut sides down, on the grill. Cook, without moving them, until they are lightly charred, about 5 minutes. Remove the tomatoes from the grill and set aside.

2. Add the onion rings to the grill. Cook, turning once halfway through cooking, until they are lightly charred, about 7 minutes. Remove from the grill and set aside. When the onion rings have cooled a little, chop them coarsely.

3. In a large pot, heat the oil over medium-low heat. Add the chopped onion and garlic and cook, stirring often, until the garlic smells good, about 2 minutes.

4. Add the grilled tomatoes, coconut milk and water. Increase the heat to medium-high and bring the soup to a boil. Reduce the heat to medium-low and simmer, uncovered, until the tomatoes are very soft and the soup smells good, 20 to 30 minutes.

5. Remove the pot from the heat and add the basil sprigs to the soup. Cover the pot and leave it for about 10 minutes to allow the basil to flavor the soup.

6. Fish out and discard the sprigs of basil, then add the sugar and salt. Using an immersion blender in the pot, blend the soup until smooth. Season with pepper to taste.

7. Ladle the soup into warm bowls and garnish with crumbled feta, a scattering of cilantro and a drizzle of avocado oil.

souper simple spinach soup

Sharon Hapton, M.S.M.
Founder and Chief Executive Officer of Soup Sisters and Broth Brothers

When my two kids were little, I made soup from spinach and potatoes. They both said it was their favorite when I asked them what recipe I should put in this book. I always made extra and delivered it to their friend Harry who lived up the street. He loved it too!

Makes about 4 servings

1 Tbsp olive oil
1 large or 2 medium leeks (white part only), chopped
1 onion, finely chopped
1 clove garlic, minced
2 cups chicken or vegetable stock
1 lb russet potatoes, peeled and cut into chunks
3 to 4 cups lightly packed fresh spinach, coarsely chopped
1 medium bunch parsley, finely chopped
½ tsp each salt and pepper
2 Tbsp softened butter (approx.)

I like to add a little ground cumin when seasoning the soup at the end, but it may not be a favorite flavor of every kid.

1. In a large pot, heat the olive oil over medium heat. Add the leek and onion and cook, stirring often, until the onion has softened, about 8 minutes. Add the garlic and cook, stirring, until it smells good, about 30 seconds.

2. Add the stock and potatoes and bring to a boil over medium-high heat. Reduce the heat to medium-low and simmer, uncovered, until the potatoes are falling apart and fork tender, 10 to 15 minutes.

3. Stir in the spinach and cook until it is wilted, about 2 minutes.

4. Remove the pot from the heat. Using an immersion blender in the pot, blend the soup until ultra-smooth. Stir in the parsley and season with salt and pepper to taste.

5. Ladle the soup into warm bowls and drop a dollop of softened butter into each serving. Yum!

creamy spicy cauliflower soup

Julie Albert and Lisa Gnat
Cookbook Authors and Bloggers, bitememore.com

What do the prize in the cereal box, an extra hour of sleep and this soup have in common? They are all bonuses, and in the case of this velvety spiced cauliflower soup, it comes in the form of having a soup that is creamy but without any cream! Not only is this warmly spiced soup healthy and hearty, it's also super simple to make.

Makes about 6 servings

2 Tbsp olive oil
1 large onion, finely chopped
2 large cloves garlic, minced
1 tsp ground cumin
1 tsp ground turmeric
½ tsp salt
½ tsp garam masala (see sidebar)
½ tsp ground ginger
¼ tsp cayenne
6½ cups vegetable stock
2 large heads cauliflower, trimmed and cut into florets
1 Tbsp fresh lemon juice
½ cup toasted slivered almonds (see sidebar)

Garam masala is a blend of spices used in South Asian cooking. The blend might include peppercorns, mace, cinnamon, cloves, cardamom and nutmeg. Look for garam masala in the spice aisle of your supermarket.

To toast almonds or other nuts, spread them out on a rimmed baking sheet and toast in a 350°F oven until golden, 5 to 6 minutes. Watch carefully as they burn quickly.

1. In a large pot, heat the olive oil over medium heat. Add the onion and cook, stirring occasionally, until the onion has softened, about 6 minutes. Stir in the garlic, cumin, turmeric, salt, garam masala, ginger and cayenne. Cook, stirring constantly, for 1 minute.

2. Add the stock and cauliflower florets and bring to a boil over medium-high heat. Reduce the heat to medium-low and simmer, uncovered, until the cauliflower is tender, about 15 minutes.

3. Remove the pot from the heat. Using an immersion blender in the pot, blend the soup until smooth. Stir in the lemon juice.

4. Ladle the soup into warm bowls, then garnish each serving with a scattering of toasted almonds.

freshii super foods soup

Annie Corrin
Age 9, Toronto, ON

This soup is full of foods which help to keep us healthy.

Makes 2 to 4 servings, but it can serve any number of people depending on the amount of ingredients you add.

4 to 6 cups vegetable stock
½ cup quinoa, rinsed and drained
¼ cup shredded kale leaves
¼ cup broccoli florets
¼ cup sliced cabbage
¼ cup sliced carrots
¼ cup sliced celery
¼ cup chopped red onion

1. Put all the ingredients in a large pot and bring to a boil over medium-high heat. Reduce the heat to medium-low and simmer, uncovered, until the quinoa and vegetables are tender, 15 to 20 minutes.

2. Ladle the soup into warm bowls and enjoy—it tastes super!

Depending on the amount of stock you add, this soup can be more or less brothy.

pappa al pomodoro

Angie Quaale
Owner of Well Seasoned, Langley, BC

In our cooking classes, we love to teach kids how to use up leftovers and create dishes that are sometimes a little bit unexpected. It is so much fun to see their enthusiasm and creativity and hear what kids think belongs in a soup pot. This soup uses up leftover French bread and is a simple dish that children can make mostly on their own or with limited supervision, depending on their age. The most often requested addition to this recipe is a grilled cheese sandwich!

Makes about 4 servings

2 Tbsp olive oil
1 large onion, finely chopped
½ tsp salt
¼ tsp red chili flakes (optional)
3 cloves garlic, minced
1 cup chicken or vegetable stock
2 lb ripe tomatoes, finely chopped

3 cups tomato juice
½ loaf day-old French bread, crusts removed and cubed
Pepper to taste
¼ cup freshly grated Parmesan cheese
10 large basil leaves, thinly sliced

This super-simple recipe can be changed in all kinds of ways:
- Experiment with other fresh herbs like rosemary, thyme, parsley or oregano.
- Turn this into a creamy soup by adding ½ cup whipping cream (35% MF) in the last 3 or 4 minutes of cooking time and stirring well to combine. (Don't use milk; when the milk reaches a boil, it will curdle.)
- If fresh tomatoes aren't available, substitute 2 cans (each 14 oz) diced tomatoes (with their juices).

1. In a large, wide pot, heat the oil over medium heat. Add the onion, salt and red chili flakes (if using) and cook, stirring often, until the onion is softened, about 10 minutes.

2. Add the garlic and cook, stirring often, until it smells good, about 3 more minutes.

3. Add the stock and bring to a boil over medium-high heat. Let bubble until the liquid has reduced by about half.

4. Add the tomatoes and return to a simmer. Reduce the heat to medium-low and simmer, uncovered, until the tomatoes are really soft and start to break down, about 15 minutes.

5. Remove the pot from the heat. Using an immersion blender in the pot, blend the soup until smooth. Return the pot to medium heat and add the tomato juice and bread cubes.

6. Simmer until the bread cubes break down completely and the soup is nice and thick, about 20 minutes. Taste the soup and add more salt and pepper to taste.

7. Ladle the soup into warm bowls and serve with the grated Parmesan and fresh basil sprinkled on top.

grandma's russian borscht

Leah Garrad-Cole
Cookbook Author and Founder of Love Child Organics, Whistler, BC

Children love helping in the kitchen. There is something heartwarming about the bonding experience of making soup together, especially if you use the time to tell them stories about their ancestors and food traditions that are special to your family.

As a child, I adored my Russian grandmother and, because of her, have deep love for Russian food. I remember watching her make borscht on several occasions and she always seemed to have a pot of this fragrant, bright red soup simmering away on her stovetop when we came to visit. My version is adapted from my grandmother's recipe, which we found scribbled on an old piece of scrap paper after she passed. Her recipe is a bit vague and the penmanship hard to decipher, but I've done my best to honor it with this recreation. The taste definitely transports me back to childhood and my grandmother's warm kitchen, so I think I've come pretty close to the original. This is for you, Grandma—know that your great-grandchildren love your borscht just as much as I did, and I've told them all about you.

Makes about 8 servings

3 medium potatoes, divided
8 cups water
¼ cup butter
1 small onion, finely chopped
2 Tbsp finely chopped seeded sweet green pepper
1 can (14 oz) diced tomatoes
3 Tbsp tomato paste
½ large green cabbage, cored and shredded
1 small beet, peeled and finely chopped
1 medium carrot, peeled and finely chopped
1 cup trimmed and finely chopped green beans
½ small cauliflower, trimmed and finely chopped
1½ tsp salt
Pepper to taste
½ cup whipping cream (35% MF)
¼ cup chopped fresh dill
Sour cream or cubed cheddar cheese for garnish

1. Peel the potatoes. Finely chop one of the potatoes and set aside for later. Cut the remaining potatoes into quarters and put them in a large pot. Add the water and bring to a boil over medium-high heat. Reduce the heat to medium-low and simmer, uncovered, until the potatoes are soft, about 15 minutes.

2. Meanwhile, melt the butter in a large skillet over medium-high heat. Add the onion and green pepper and cook, stirring often, until the onion has softened, about 5 minutes.

3. Add the tomatoes (with their juices), tomato paste and half of the cabbage to the skillet. Reduce the heat to medium and cook, stirring often, until the cabbage is tender, for 10 minutes or so.

4. When the boiled potatoes are ready, use a slotted spoon to remove them from the pot (leave the water in the pot). Put the potatoes in a bowl and mash them until smooth.

5. Return the mashed potatoes to the pot of water, then add the tomato and vegetable mixture from the skillet. Add the rest of the cabbage to the pot, along with the beet, carrot, beans, cauliflower, reserved chopped potato, salt and a few grindings of pepper. Bring to a boil over medium-high heat. Reduce the heat to medium and simmer, uncovered, until all the vegetables are tender, about 10 minutes.

6. Stir in the cream and dill and adjust the seasonings to your taste.

7. Ladle the soup into warm bowls and serve topped with sour cream, or do as we do in our family and stir cubed cheddar cheese right into the soup.

sneaky carrot-ginger soup

Daniel Wagner
Chef and Owner, Rain City Soups, Vancouver, BC

Kid approved many times over (just don't mention the turnips)! Fun to make and fun to eat.

Makes about 6 servings

5 lb carrots, peeled and chopped
2 large onions, chopped
3 stalks celery, chopped
3 cloves garlic
2 purple turnips, peeled and chopped
2-inch piece fresh ginger, peeled and sliced into rounds
1 can (14 oz) coconut milk
¼ cup packed brown sugar
1 cinnamon stick
Ground nutmeg to taste
Salt and pepper to taste
Water as needed

1. Place all the ingredients, except the water, in a large pot. Add enough water to cover the vegetables. Bring to a boil over medium-high heat, stirring often.

2. Reduce the heat to medium-low and simmer the soup, uncovered and stirring occasionally, until all the vegetables are very soft, about 30 minutes.

3. Remove the pot from the heat. Fish out and discard the cinnamon stick, then, using an immersion blender in the pot, blend the soup until smooth. Season with salt and pepper to taste, then ladle into warm bowls. Or let cool completely, chill in the fridge and serve icy cold.

summer-fresh roasted tomato soup

David Hawksworth
Chef and Owner of Hawksworth, Vancouver, BC

I love this soup, especially during the summer months when tomatoes are at their peak. If you can find flavorful heirloom tomatoes when they are in season, use those instead of Roma. This soup is ideal if your guests have dietary issues, as it is both dairy- and gluten-free.

Makes about 4 servings

6½ lb Roma tomatoes, cored and cut in half lengthwise
1 cup granulated sugar
6½ Tbsp salt
Olive oil to taste
1 Tbsp canola oil
2 large onions, chopped
1½ large carrots, peeled and chopped
1½ bulbs fennel, cored and chopped

2½ stalks celery, chopped
4 cloves garlic, coarsely chopped
½ to 1 red bird's eye chili, according to taste, stem removed
2 cups tomato paste
Water as needed
¼ bunch parsley
¼ bunch basil
Salt and pepper to taste

1. Preheat the oven to 250°F. Put the tomatoes in a large baking dish. Sprinkle the sugar and salt over the tomatoes, then drizzle with olive oil. Stir to combine everything well. Bake, uncovered, for 10 hours or overnight until the tomatoes are very tender. Remove from the oven and set aside.

2. In a large pot over medium-high heat, heat the canola oil. Add the onions, carrots, fennel, celery, garlic and chili, then cook, stirring often, until the vegetables begin to brown, about 10 minutes.

3. Add the tomato paste, then cook for another 5 minutes until the paste is dark and smells good.

4. Add the cooked tomatoes with all their juices from the dish. Pour in just enough water to cover the vegetables. Bring it all to a boil over medium-high heat. Reduce the heat to medium-low and simmer, uncovered, until all the vegetables are tender, 30 to 45 minutes.

5. Remove the pot from the heat and add the parsley and basil. Using an immersion blender in the pot, blend the soup until smooth. Pour the soup through a fine-mesh sieve set over a clean pot. Reheat the soup over medium heat, then season with salt and pepper to taste. Ladle the soup into warm soup bowls and serve.

squash 'n' coconut soup with maple

Kelly Childs and Erinn Weatherbie

Cookbook Authors and Co-owners of Kelly's Bake Shoppe and Lettuce Love Café, Burlington, ON

Doesn't this soup sound warm and soothing? Butternut squash roasts to a melting sweetness that's emphasized by the maple syrup and coconut milk. This is a great choice for kids, especially if they're veggie-averse. The flavor will squash any reluctance!

Makes about 10 servings

5 Tbsp olive oil, divided
2 large butternut squash
½ tsp ground cinnamon
2 medium onions, finely chopped
½ tsp red chili flakes
6 cloves garlic, minced

2 Tbsp minced fresh ginger
1 tsp salt
8 cups vegetable stock
½ cup canned coconut milk
2 Tbsp maple syrup

When the squash is ready, it will be very easy to scoop out of its skin, so make sure you roast it until it's very soft. The soup can be refrigerated for up to 5 days and freezes well.

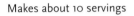

1. Preheat the oven to 375°F. Brush two baking sheets or roasting pans with some of the olive oil.

2. Cut the squash in half and scoop out the seeds. Lightly brush the cut side of each squash half with a little of the remaining olive oil and sprinkle with the cinnamon. Place the squash, cut sides down, on the baking sheets and cover tightly with foil. Bake until the squash has softened, 45 to 60 minutes.

3. Meanwhile, heat the remaining olive oil in a large pot over medium heat. Add the onions and cook, stirring often, until the onions are translucent, about 3 minutes. Add the red chili flakes and cook, stirring often, for 3 more minutes. Add the garlic, ginger and salt and cook, stirring often, until the garlic mixture smells good, about 2 minutes. Remove the pot from the heat.

4. When the squash is ready, remove it from the oven and let it cool for 15 minutes. Using a large spoon, scoop the squash out of its skin and add to the pot, along with the vegetable stock.

5. Return the pot to medium heat and bring the soup to a simmer. Simmer, uncovered, for about 15 minutes to allow the flavors to combine and deepen. Add the coconut milk and maple syrup.

6. Remove the pot from the heat. Using an immersion blender in the pot, blend the soup until smooth. Ladle the soup into warm bowls and enjoy.

This recipe is adapted from Made with Love *(Appetite by Random House, 2016).*

autumn pear (or apple) and parsnip soup

Julie Van Rosendaal
Cookbook Author, CBC Radio Food Columnist and Blogger, dinnerwithjulie.com

In the fall, ripe pears add sweetness and fragrance to parsnip soup. It's a great way to use up overripe pears, but tart apples are delicious as well. I love a smooth, sippable soup I can pour into an insulated to-go cup and take with me. My son Willem isn't a fan of parsnips, but likes to do the puréeing using a hand-held immersion blender, right in the pot.

Makes about 4 servings

Canola oil
1 onion, chopped
2 cloves garlic, peeled
4 cups chicken or vegetable stock
2 cups water
3 large parsnips, peeled and chopped
1 large ripe pear or tart apple, cored and chopped
2 tsp fresh thyme leaves
1 cup whipping cream (35% MF) or half-and-half cream (10% MF)
Salt and pepper to taste

1. In a medium pot, heat a drizzle of oil over medium-high heat. Add the onion and cook, stirring often, until it is softened, 4 to 5 minutes. Crush the garlic cloves with the flat side of a large knife. Add the garlic to the pot and cook for another minute.

2. Add the stock, water, parsnips, pear (or apple) and thyme. Increase the heat to medium-high and bring to a boil. Reduce the heat to medium-low and simmer, uncovered, until the parsnips are very soft, 20 to 30 minutes.

3. Add the cream, and season with salt and pepper to taste. Remove the pot from the heat. Using an immersion blender in the pot, blend the soup until smooth.

4. Ladle the soup into warm bowls and enjoy.

If you omit the cream and use vegetable stock, this soup is suitable for vegans.

a jack-o'-lantern you can eat (easy pumpkin soup)

Ruth Reichl
Author and Former Editor-in-Chief of *Gourmet*

I was pretty much a kid myself when I invented this dish. Wandering through the farmers' market on a glorious fall day, I spotted a fat, round, orange pumpkin and thought what a perfect soup bowl it would make. And then I thought: it could be the soup too! This is a very hearty soup; add a salad and you have a substantial meal.

Makes about 8 servings

1 small pumpkin (about 7 lb) with a flat bottom
½ tsp salt
½ tsp pepper
½ lb baguette (about two-thirds of a narrow baguette)
1 cup chicken or vegetable stock
1½ cups whipping cream (35% MF)
6 oz Gruyère cheese, coarsely grated
6 oz Emmental cheese, coarsely grated
1 Tbsp grapeseed oil
Roasted pumpkin seeds for garnish (recipe opposite)

1. Preheat the oven to 400°F.

2. Cut a small circle about 3 inches in diameter off the top of the pumpkin, as if you were about to carve a jack-o'-lantern, and scrape out all the seeds and fibers with a large spoon. Reserve the seeds for roasting (recipe opposite). Sprinkle the inside of the pumpkin with the salt and pepper.

3. Slice the baguette into ½-inch slices and toast them on both sides until golden brown.

4. In a small bowl, whisk the stock and cream together until well combined. In another small bowl, stir together the two cheeses.

5. Now comes the fun part. Put a layer of toasted bread in the pumpkin and cover it with about 1 cup of the cheese and ½ cup of the stock mixture. Continue layering the ingredients in the same order until the pumpkin is almost full and there is only about a ½-inch space at the top. Depending on the shape of your pumpkin, you may have some bread and cheese left over but use all the stock mixture.

6. Put the top back on the pumpkin, then brush the entire pumpkin with the oil. Carefully lift the pumpkin into a large baking dish, then bake until the pumpkin is tender when pierced with a slim knife, about 1½ hours.

7. To serve, scoop the filling into bowls, along with the soft flesh of the pumpkin, and garnish with the roasted pumpkin seeds.

This recipe is adapted from Ruth's first cookbook Mmmmm: A Feastiary *(Holt Rinehart and Winston, 1972).*

roasted pumpkin seeds

1. Put the pumpkin seeds in a large sieve, then rinse them under cold running water until they no longer feel sticky. Pick out and discard any stringy pieces of pumpkin.

2. Spread the rinsed seeds in a single layer on one or two large baking sheets, then set aside to dry thoroughly, stirring and separating the seeds once or twice.

3. Heat a large dry cast iron skillet over medium heat. Add the pumpkin seeds and cook, stirring, until they become slightly puffy. Splash on a bit of olive oil and sprinkle with salt. These make a nice snack and a very good garnish for the pumpkin soup.

go wild mushroom soup

Nora Pouillon
Author and Chef and Owner of Restaurant Nora, Washington, DC

This is one of our family favorites. My mother often made it after we went mushroom hunting in the woods in the Austrian countryside near where I grew up.

Makes about 4 servings

2 Tbsp olive oil
3 Tbsp finely chopped onion
1 tsp minced garlic
1 lb assorted wild mushrooms, such as chanterelle, oyster, porcini, shiitake, cremini
    and/or portobello, sliced
2 stalks celery, thinly sliced
1 small leek (white part only), thinly sliced
1 carrot, peeled and thinly sliced
3 cups vegetable or chicken stock
1 Tbsp tamari (see sidebar)
Salt and pepper to taste
2 Tbsp crème fraîche, sour cream or whipped cream (35% MF)
1 ½ Tbsp chopped parsley or fresh tarragon

1. In a large saucepan, heat the oil over medium heat. Add the onion and cook, stirring often, until the onion has softened, about 4 minutes. Add the garlic and cook to soften.

2. Add the mushrooms, celery, leek and carrot. Cook, stirring often, until the mushrooms start to soften, about 4 minutes.

3. Add stock and tamari and bring to a boil over medium-high heat. Reduce the heat to medium-low and simmer, covered, until all the vegetables are tender, about 10 to 15 minutes.

4. Remove the pot from the heat and cool the soup. Using a blender, a food processor or an immersion blender, blend the soup until smooth. Season with salt and pepper to taste.

5. Reheat to serve. Ladle the soup into warm bowls. Garnish each serving with a dollop of crème fraîche and sprinkle with chopped parsley.

Tamari is a type of Japanese soy sauce without wheat, making it gluten free. If you can't find it in the Asian section of your supermarket, substitute regular soy sauce.

We often make this soup at my restaurant, Nora, when we have accumulated enough trimmings and stems left over from our other wild mushroom dishes; that way we don't waste any food and we make economical use of the trimmings. To enhance the mushroom flavor even more, soak some dried porcini for 20 minutes, then drain and add to the soup along with the fresh mushrooms.

yummy broccoli and cashew soup

Sarah Britton
Cookbook Author and Blogger, mynewroots.org

Although I've made it a habit to cover up the taste of broccoli more often than letting its true flavor shine through, this soup is different. First of all, it's mostly broccoli, and yet it is still scrumptious. It doesn't hide underneath crazy cheese sauce or dressing because it doesn't need to! It's rich and creamy, with a hint of spice that you can dial up or down depending on whom you're cooking for.

I used cashews to deliver that unctuous richness, and nutritional yeast to mimic the taste of dairy. Not only does this take the soup to a whole other level, but swirling that velvety cream through the bowl of green creates a beguilingly beautiful result—and it's fun for little kids to do.

Makes about 6 servings

If you want to use the stems of the broccoli for this soup (waste not want not!), add them to the pot and cook them for 2 to 3 minutes before adding the florets. Remember, too, that the broccoli leaves are completely edible and loaded with nutrients.

cashew cream
1 cup raw cashews
1 ¼ cups water
1 ¼ tsp salt, divided
2 cloves garlic
2 tsp fresh lemon juice

soup
2 Tbsp coconut oil
1 lb onions, chopped
½ tsp salt
6 cloves garlic, minced
Minced green chili to taste
6 cups vegetable stock
2 lb broccoli florets (see sidebar)
1 cup packed parsley leaves and tender stems
½ cup nutritional yeast (see page 111)
2 tsp fresh lemon juice
Salt and pepper to taste
Red chili flakes for garnish (optional)

1. For the cashew cream, place the cashews in a large bowl and add the water. Stir in 1 tsp salt, then let soak at room temperature for about 4 hours or overnight. Drain and rinse the cashews.

2. To a countertop blender, add the cashews, garlic, lemon juice and the remaining salt. Blend on high speed until the mixture is completely smooth. Season with more salt to taste. Scrape out half of the cashew cream into a bowl and set aside. Leave the rest of the cashew cream in the blender.

3. In a large pot, heat the coconut oil over medium heat. Add the onions and salt, and cook, stirring often, until the onions have softened, about 8 minutes. Add the garlic and green chili and cook, stirring, until it smells good, about 2 minutes.

4. Add the stock and bring to a boil over medium-high heat. Add the broccoli and simmer for just 5 minutes. Do not overcook; the broccoli should be bright green and not completely tender.

5. Add some of the soup to the cashew cream in the blender. Holding the lid on firmly, blend on high speed until smooth. Add the parsley, nutritional yeast and lemon juice to the blender. Blend again on high speed until smooth. Pour the blended soup into a clean pot. Blend the remaining soup in batches, adding each blended batch to the pot.

6. Reheat the soup over medium heat. Season with salt and pepper to taste. Ladle the soup into warm bowls. Add a few spoonfuls of the reserved cashew cream to each bowl, then swirl it into the soup. Sprinkle with red chili flakes (if using) and a couple of parsley leaves and serve.

smiley face carrot soup

Rogelio Herrera
Chef and Owner, Alloy, Calgary, AB

My sous chef Adam and I wanted to come up with a soup for kids that was not only healthy but fun. Carrot and ginger is a yummy combo and decorating each bowl with a smiley face will tempt the pickiest of eaters. Older kids can help cook while the younger ones can design the happy faces.

Makes about 6 servings

soup
2 Tbsp olive oil
5 lb carrots, peeled and chopped
1 cup chopped onion
2 Tbsp ground ginger
½ Tbsp ground turmeric
8 cups cold water
4 cups canned coconut milk
Salt to taste

for the smiley faces
1 cup Greek yogurt in a squeeze bottle
Parsley leaves
Olive oil in a squeeze bottle
Paprika

Ginger and turmeric are known to help with inflammation, and carrots—packed with lots of vitamins and minerals—are an excellent immune booster.

1. In a large pot, heat the olive oil over medium heat. Add the carrots and onion and cook, stirring often, until the onion has softened, about 8 minutes.

2. Add the ginger and turmeric and cook, stirring often, until the carrots and onions are coated with the spices and they smell good, about 2 minutes.

3. Add the water, coconut milk and salt to taste, then bring to a boil over medium-high heat. Reduce the heat to low and simmer, uncovered, for 1 hour, stirring every 10 minutes or so to prevent the carrots from sticking to the bottom of the pot.

4. Remove the pot from the heat. Using an immersion blender in the pot, blend the soup until smooth. For a silky smooth soup, pour it through a fine-mesh sieve set over a clean pot. Season with salt to taste.

5. Ladle the soup into warm bowls. Use the squeeze bottle of yogurt to draw the best smiley face you can on the surface of each serving of soup. Add parsley leaves for hair, dots of olive oil for freckles and sprinklings of paprika for rosy cheeks.

french onion soup with parmesan garlic bread

Lynn Crawford
Chef and Owner, Ruby Watchco, Toronto, ON

There's nothing cozier than the rich smell of French onion soup simmering in the kitchen. The aroma instantly brings me back to the first time I had it at a restaurant. I was a young child and recall the heat radiating from the bowl, the smell and how it made me feel comforted. Once I took my first taste, I was hooked. I remember constantly begging my mother to make it at home.

This is a very traditional French onion soup recipe and I encourage you to try it and create your own memories with your family and loved ones. Don't be discouraged by the quantity of onions—once cooked down and caramelized, they develop a rich, buttery flavor. The Swiss cheese and golden toasted Parmesan garlic bread add gooeyness and crunch. Enjoy!

Makes about 6 servings

2 Tbsp olive oil
2 Tbsp unsalted butter
6 large Vidalia onions, halved from pole to pole then cut into ¼-inch slices
3 Tbsp granulated sugar
2 cloves garlic, minced
2 sprigs fresh thyme
1 bay leaf
6 cups beef stock
1 cup dry white wine
¼ cup Cognac (optional)
Salt and pepper to taste
Parmesan Garlic Bread (recipe follows)
8 ounces Gruyère cheese, shredded

1. In a large heavy-bottomed pot, heat the oil and butter over medium heat. Add the onions, sugar, garlic, thyme and bay leaf. Cook, stirring occasionally, until the onions have started to darken at the edges, about 15 minutes.

2. Reduce the temperature to low and leave the onions to caramelize, uncovered and stirring occasionally, until the bottom of the pot is covered with a rich, dark, nutty brown film, about 1 hour.

If you use vegetable stock instead of beef stock, this soup is suitable for vegetarians.

3. Add the stock and wine and bring to a simmer. Simmer, stirring occasionally, for 15 minutes. Fish out and discard the thyme sprigs and bay leaf. Add the cognac (if using) and season with salt and pepper to taste.

4. Preheat the broiler to high. Set six onion soup or other ovenproof bowls on a large rimmed baking sheet. Ladle the soup into the bowls. Arrange three pieces of Parmesan garlic bread (recipe follows) in a fan shape on top of each portion of soup. Sprinkle each with a generous handful of Gruyère cheese.

5. Place the baking sheet with the bowls about 4 inches from the broiler and broil until the cheese melts and is golden, about 5 minutes. Serve immediately.

parmesan garlic bread

½ cup freshly grated Parmesan cheese
½ cup mayonnaise
2 Tbsp finely chopped chives
2 Tbsp minced garlic
1 Tbsp Sriracha hot sauce
1 narrow baguette, cut in half lengthwise

1. Preheat the oven to 350°F.

2. In a medium bowl, stir together the Parmesan, mayonnaise, chives, garlic and Sriracha until a smooth paste forms.

3. Spread the Parmesan mixture onto the cut sides of the baguette. Place the baguette halves, cheese side up, on a large rimmed, parchment-lined baking sheet. Bake on the center rack of the oven until golden, about 15 minutes.

4. When cool enough to handle, cut each baguette half diagonally into small pieces.

totally tubular tomato soup

Karen Anderson
President of Alberta Food Tours Inc.

If you omit the cream, this soup is suitable for vegans.

Umami is the so-called fifth taste (after sweet, salty, sour and bitter) and adds rich, meaty flavor. Look for umami paste in the spice aisle of your supermarket.

Totally Tubular Mediterranean Seafood Soup
Follow the recipe, omitting the cream and using 1 tsp (or 1 squeeze) of anchovy paste in place of the tomato paste. Before heating the soup, add 1 can (14 oz) of baby clams (undrained) and 1 Tbsp of drained capers.

Soup was the first thing I taught my son to make. We roasted tomatoes, red peppers, garlic and onion until they were nicely caramelized, then threw the whole works into a blender. From there it got fun. My young son had learned to use a can opener and blender that day so instead of moving on to chopping we went totally tubular for the rest of our ingredients. I lined up a row of ingredients in squeeze tubes (I love packing food in squeeze tubes for camping trips and had lots left over from the summer). My son chose peppery harissa, rich tomato paste and a brightly flavored pesto and enjoyed squeezing dollops of each into the pot. He has loved making soup ever since. Once you've gone totally tubular, inspiration is only a squeeze away. This simpler version of the soup we made that day uses canned tomatoes but lots of squeeze tubes!

Makes about 2 servings

1 can (28 oz) whole tomatoes
½ cup half-and-half cream (10% MF; optional)
1 Tbsp tomato or umami paste (see sidebar) or 2 squeezes from a tube
1 tsp basil or sun-dried tomato pesto or 1 squeeze from a tube
1 tsp garlic paste or 1 squeeze from a tube
Salt and pepper to taste

1. Tip the tomatoes and their juices into a food processor or blender and pulse them by switching the appliance on and off until the tomatoes are smooth.

2. Add the cream (if using), tomato paste, pesto and garlic paste, then pulse the blender until the ingredients are well combined.

3. Pour the soup into a large pot. Cook over medium heat, stirring occasionally, until the soup is hot enough to serve.

4. Season the soup with salt and pepper to taste, then ladle into warm bowls and enjoy.

spicy thai carrot soup

Teagan Young
Age 13, Calgary, AB

I like this soup because its flavors are from another country and it is simple to make. You can make it spicy if you want.

Makes about 8 servings

2 Tbsp olive oil
2 medium onions, chopped
6 cloves garlic, minced
2 lb carrots, peeled and chopped
1 Tbsp minced fresh ginger
2 tsp chili-garlic paste (see sidebar)
4 cups vegetable or chicken stock
1 Tbsp fresh lime juice
3 Tbsp smooth peanut butter
1 tsp dark sesame oil
1 can (14 oz) coconut milk
Salt and pepper to taste

Look for Thai chili-garlic paste in the Asian section of your supermarket.

1. In a large pot, heat the oil over medium heat. Add the onions and cook, stirring often, until they start to soften, about 5 minutes. Add the garlic and cook, stirring often, until it smells good, about 2 minutes.

2. Add the carrots, ginger and chili-garlic paste to the pot. Cook, stirring often, until the edges of the carrots start to soften, about 5 minutes.

3. Add the stock and bring to a boil over medium-high heat. Reduce the heat to medium-low and simmer, uncovered, until the carrots are soft, about 20 minutes. Stir in the lime juice, peanut butter and sesame oil.

4. Remove the pot from the heat. Using an immersion blender in the pot, blend the soup until smooth.

5. Stir in the coconut milk. Heat the soup over low heat, then season with salt and pepper to taste.

6. Ladle the soup into warm bowls then dig into its spiciness.

roasted pumpkin soup with warm brie crostini

Michael Noble
Chef/Proprietor at NOtaBLE and The Nash Restaurants, Calgary, AB

This soup reminds me of simple times when my children were young, but were already soup lovers! There's nothing better than a hot bowl of soup, some crusty bread and delicious cheese to bring a family together.

Makes about 8 servings

1 small pumpkin (3 to 5 lb)
7 Tbsp olive oil, divided
2 Tbsp finely chopped fresh thyme leaves
2 Tbsp salt
1 tsp ground cloves
1 tsp pepper
½ tsp ground cinnamon
2 Tbsp butter
2 onions, finely chopped
4 cloves garlic, minced
2 stalks celery, finely chopped
2 carrots, peeled and finely chopped
1 navel orange, zested and juiced
1 cup white wine (optional)
Salt and pepper to taste
8 cups chicken or vegetable stock
1 cup whipping cream (35% MF)
Warm Brie Crostini (recipe opposite)

1. Preheat the oven to 375°F.

2. Cut the pumpkin in half and scoop out the seeds with a large spoon. Cut the pumpkin into large pieces, leaving the rind on. In a large bowl, toss the pumpkin pieces with 5 Tbsp of the olive oil, thyme, salt, cloves, pepper and cinnamon. Arrange the pumpkin pieces, skin side down, on a large rimmed baking sheet. Bake until the pumpkin is very tender and browned, 45 to 60 minutes.

3. Remove the pumpkin from the oven and let it cool. With a large spoon, scoop all of the flesh from the pumpkin pieces, discarding the rind. Chop the pumpkin flesh and set it aside for later.

4. In a large pot, heat the remaining oil and the butter over medium heat. Once the butter is bubbly and melted, add the onions and garlic. Cook, stirring often, until the onions are translucent, about 7 minutes.

5. Add the celery and carrots and cook, stirring often, until the celery starts to soften, about 7 more minutes.

6. Add the orange zest and cook, stirring, until it smells good, about 1 minute.

7. Add the white wine (if using), the juice from the orange and salt and pepper to taste. Bring to a boil over medium-high heat. Reduce the heat to medium-low and simmer, stirring often, until all the liquid has almost completely evaporated, 5 to 7 minutes.

8. Add the stock and bring to a boil over medium-high heat. Reduce the heat to medium-low and simmer the soup, uncovered, until all the vegetables are tender, about 40 minutes.

9. Add the reserved roasted pumpkin to the pot and bring back to a simmer for 10 minutes.

10. Remove the pot from the heat. Using an immersion blender in the pot, blend the soup until smooth. For a silky smooth soup, pour it through a fine-mesh sieve set over a clean pot.

11. Add the cream and reheat the soup over medium heat. Season with more salt and pepper to taste. Ladle the soup into warm bowls and serve with the warm brie crostini (recipe follows) either floating on the top of each serving of soup or on the side.

warm brie crostini

Makes about 20 crostini

1 day-old narrow baguette
Extra virgin olive oil as required
6 oz brie, thinly sliced

1. Preheat the oven to 350°F.

2. Cut the baguette into 1-inch slices and arrange in a single layer on a large baking sheet. Drizzle evenly with olive oil. Bake until the slices are light golden brown, 7 to 8 minutes.

3. Place a slice of brie on each baguette slice. Put the baking sheet back in the oven until the cheese has melted, about 3 minutes.

butternut-coconut soup with sumac sprinkle

Toni Profera
Soup Sister, Cookbook Author, Health Coach and Blogger, toniprofera.com

This soup has become a family favorite and pairs very well with a crisp arugula salad with a nice lemon and pepper dressing in an olive oil base.

I like a very smooth and rather brothy soup, so I use a countertop blender, but some people prefer it thick. If you're in the latter camp, reduce the amount of stock to 4 cups and stick with the immersion blender.

Sumac is a spice with a tart, lemony flavor used in Middle Eastern cooking. Look for it online or in the spice aisle of larger supermarkets or ethnic grocery stores.

Makes about 6 servings

1 large butternut squash
2 Tbsp ghee or olive oil, or a combination of the two
1 large onion, coarsely chopped
1 sweet yellow pepper, seeded and coarsely chopped
1 large shallot, coarsely chopped
2 cloves garlic, minced (optional)
1 small piece fresh ginger, minced
1 tsp ground turmeric
½ tsp ground coriander
Pinch of white pepper

Salt to taste
5½ cups chicken or vegetable stock
1 can (14 oz) coconut milk (preferably organic)
Juice of 1 lime, plus more for serving
1 small bunch cilantro, finely chopped
Sumac to taste (see sidebar)
Crumbled goat milk feta cheese for garnish (optional)
Sriracha hot pepper sauce for garnish (optional)

1. Preheat the oven to 350°F. Use a metal skewer to poke some holes in the squash. Place in a baking dish and bake until it softens up just a bit, about 20 minutes. (Baking the squash makes it much easier and safer to peel and slice.) Remove the squash from the oven and set it aside to cool.

2. Cut the squash in half and scoop out the seeds with a large spoon. Peel the squash and cut the flesh into cubes. Set aside to use later.

3. In a large pot, melt the ghee over medium heat. Add the onion, yellow pepper, shallot, garlic (if using) and ginger and cook, stirring often, until the onion starts to soften, about 5 minutes. Add the squash and cook, stirring often, for 3 or 4 minutes.

4. Add the turmeric, coriander, pepper and a little salt and cook, stirring, until it smells good, about 1 minute.

5. Add the stock and coconut milk and bring to a boil over medium-high heat.

Reduce the heat to medium-low and simmer, uncovered, until the vegetables are tender, about 20 minutes. Stir in the lime juice.

6. Remove the pot from the heat. Using an immersion blender in the pot, blend the soup until smooth. If using the full blender, put back into the pot and bring to a simmer.

7. Ladle the soup into warm bowls and garnish each serving with a scattering of cilantro and sumac and a squeeze of lime. Add a drift of crumbled feta and a dash of Sriracha for extra zip (if using).

tomato-potato soup with roasted garlic

Shamus Faulkner
Age 12, Kelowna, BC

You say tomato, I say potato. Either way, I like how delicious and smooth this soup is. And sometimes it has a kick if you put in too much cayenne! My friends and neighbors tried my experimental soup and they all loved it.

Makes about 6 servings

1 Tbsp olive oil
1 medium onion, chopped
3 stalks celery, chopped
4 cups vegetable or chicken stock
1 can (28 oz) diced tomatoes
2 large potatoes, peeled and chopped

½ tsp each salt and pepper
1 whole head Roasted Garlic
  (see page 163)
2 Tbsp honey
½ tsp cayenne (optional)

The special ingredient in this soup is the roasted garlic. Ask a grown-up to roast the head of garlic for you.

1. In a medium pot, heat the oil over medium heat. Add the onion and celery and cook, stirring often, until the onion starts to soften, about 4 minutes.

2. Add the stock, tomatoes (with their juices), potatoes and salt and pepper. Bring to a boil over medium-high heat. Reduce the heat to medium-low and simmer, uncovered, until the vegetables are tender, about 20 minutes.

3. Remove the pot from the heat. Using an immersion blender in the pot, blend the soup until smooth.

4. Bring the soup back to a boil over medium-high heat. Add the roasted garlic cloves, honey and cayenne (if using). Stir well or, for a smoother soup, blend again with the immersion blender.

5. Ladle the soup into warm bowls and enjoy its garlicky goodness.

chèvre onion soup

Matthew Sherback
Age 12, Calgary, AB

I study French at school so that's why I use the French word for goat cheese (*chèvre*), but you could also call this "French Onion Soup with Goat Cheese". It is the first soup I learned to make and my grandma and mom taught me. My mom's friend Janice Beaton brings cheese over when she comes for dinner. I like her cheese. I thought adding cheese to my grandma's soup would be fun. You can make it without goat cheese, but if you want to make it special, put the cheese in.

Makes about 8 servings

1 cup butter	4 cups whole milk (3.25% MF)
10 cups coarsely chopped onions	1 lb soft, unripened goat cheese
2 Tbsp salt	1 cup half-and-half cream (10% MF)
3 sprigs thyme	3 Tbsp granulated sugar
2 bay leaves	Croutons or crusty bread to serve
4 whole black peppercorns	

1. In a large pot, melt the butter over medium heat. Add the onions and salt and cook, stirring occasionally, until the onions are very tender and sweet but not caramelized, about 20 minutes.

2. Make a bouquet garni by tying the thyme, bay leaves and peppercorns in a square of cheesecloth. Add it to the pot, along with the milk.

3. Bring the soup to a boil over medium-high heat. Reduce the heat to low and simmer, partially covered, for about 1 hour. Fish out and discard the bouquet garni.

4. Whisk the goat cheese into the soup until it melts. Add the half-and-half cream and sugar.

5. Remove the pot from the heat. Using an immersion blender in the pot, blend the soup until smooth. Pour through a fine-mesh sieve set over a clean pot. Reheat over medium heat.

6. Ladle the soup into warm bowls and scatter croutons over the top, or serve with crusty bread on the side.

green monster soup

Sam Turnbull

Cookbook Author and Blogger, *itdoesnttastelikechicken.com*

As a kid, every spring I would wander into the forest and find the patch of wild leeks that grew there. I loved eating raw leeks as a snack—weird kid, I know—then I would collect a big bag of them and help my mom make a giant pot of green soup. (And by "help my mom," I mean drop off the leeks and go back into the forest to play until it got dark.)

Wild leeks aren't easy to find, but you can get all of the same forest flavors from your local grocery store. This soup is like spring by the spoonful: rich, earthy, creamy and brilliant green. It's the perfect shade of green for monsters, and the perfect way to woo your kids into eating more greens.

Makes about 8 servings

1 Tbsp olive oil
2 leeks (pale green and white parts only), thinly sliced
2 cloves garlic, minced
6 cups vegetable stock
1 head broccoli, coarsely chopped
1 russet potato, peeled and coarsely chopped
6 oz baby spinach
1 cup canned coconut milk (not light)
½ tsp salt
¼ tsp pepper

1. In a large pot, heat the olive oil over medium heat. Add the leeks and garlic and cook, stirring often, until the leeks have softened and are beginning to brown, about 5 minutes.

2. Add the stock, broccoli and potato, and bring to a boil over medium-high heat. Reduce the heat to medium-low and simmer, uncovered, until the broccoli is fork tender, 10 to 15 minutes. Stir in the spinach and cook 1 more minute until the spinach wilts into the soup.

3. Remove the pot from the heat. Using an immersion blender in the pot, blend the soup until smooth and creamy.

4. Stir in the coconut milk and season with salt and pepper to taste. Ladle the soup into warm bowls and enjoy a taste of spring.

tuscan tomato bread soup with poached egg

Julie Albert and Lisa Gnat
Cookbook Authors and Bloggers, bitememore.com

Head to Tuscany without leaving home with this hearty, simple and super-flavorful soup. Topped with a poached egg, this is the ultimate comfort food: a healthy meal-in-a-bowl that would make any nonna proud.

Makes 6 servings

1 can (28 oz) whole tomatoes (preferably San Marzano)
2 Tbsp olive oil
1 large onion, chopped
2 large cloves garlic, minced
Pinch of red chili flakes
½ cup dry white wine
2 Tbsp tomato paste
1 tsp granulated sugar

½ tsp salt
¼ tsp pepper
6 cups chicken or vegetable stock
6 cups cubed day-old rustic bread
6 Tbsp thinly sliced fresh basil leaves
¼ cup white vinegar
6 large eggs
1 cup shaved Parmesan cheese
Extra virgin olive oil for drizzling

1. Tip the tomatoes and their juices into a medium bowl. Using a potato masher or a large fork, crush the tomatoes. Set aside for later.

2. In a large pot, heat the oil over medium heat. Add the onion and cook, stirring often, until softened, about 8 minutes. Add the garlic and red chili flakes and cook, stirring constantly, until they smell good, about 1 minute. Add the wine and let bubble until it has almost all evaporated, about 2 minutes.

3. Add the reserved crushed tomatoes, tomato paste, sugar, salt and pepper. Bring to a simmer over medium heat. Reduce the heat to low and simmer, uncovered and stirring occasionally, for 10 minutes. Add the stock, bread and 2 Tbsp of the sliced basil. Simmer for 20 more minutes.

4. Just before you serve the soup, combine 2 cups of water and the vinegar in a wide saucepan and bring to a simmer over medium heat. Crack one egg into a small bowl and carefully slide the egg into the water. Repeat with the remaining eggs. Let the eggs poach, uncovered, just until the whites are set, about 3 minutes.

5. Meanwhile, ladle the soup into warm bowls. Using a slotted spoon, carefully remove the poached eggs from the water and place one in each bowl of soup.

6. Scatter each bowl of soup with shaved Parmesan cheese and the rest of the sliced basil, then drizzle with olive oil. Serve immediately.

pumpkin-pie-spiced carrot soup

Aston Hemming
Age 6, London, ON

My mom is the cookbook author Carolyn Hemming (*Quinoa 365*; *Quinoa Revolution*, etc.). This soup is made with nutritious carrots, sweetened with maple syrup and spiced up so like pumpkin pie, your friends and family will swear it's pumpkin soup! This gluten-free, vegetarian, veggie-packed autumn soup is "pumpkin-pie" tasty enough to make all year round.

Makes about 2 servings

1 Tbsp butter or grapeseed oil	½ tsp ground ginger
½ cup chopped onion	¼ tsp ground nutmeg
4 cups peeled, chopped carrots	Pinch of ground cloves
4 cups vegetable stock	¼ cup plain yogurt or kefir (optional; see sidebar)
3 Tbsp maple syrup	
1½ tsp fresh lemon juice	4 candied pecans (optional)
¼ tsp salt	Ground cinnamon for garnish (optional)
1 tsp ground cinnamon	

1. In a large pot, heat the butter over medium heat. Add the onion and cook, stirring often, until the onion is translucent, about 4 minutes.

2. Add the carrots and cook, stirring often, until the edges of carrots begin to soften, about 4 minutes. Add the stock and bring to a boil over medium-high heat. Cook, uncovered, until the carrots are tender, 5 to 6 minutes. Reduce the heat to medium-low and simmer, uncovered, until the carrots are completely softened, 5 to 10 more minutes.

3. Remove the pot from the heat. Using an immersion blender in the pot, blend the soup until smooth.

4. Return the pot to medium heat and reheat the soup if necessary. Stir in the maple syrup, lemon juice, salt, cinnamon, ginger, nutmeg and cloves.

5. Ladle the soup into warm bowls and add a swirl of plain yogurt or kefir (if using) to the middle of each serving, then garnish with a candied pecan and an extra sprinkle of cinnamon, if you like. Enjoy!

Kefir is a tangy, refreshing fermented milk beverage. Look for it in the dairy aisle of your supermarket.

Make this soup vegan-friendly by using grapeseed oil instead of butter and omitting the yogurt or kefir.

posh-tasting red pepper and coconut soup

Taya Groner
Age 9, Vancouver, BC

This soup is really yummy and creamy. It totally tastes like it was made in a fancy restaurant and is super easy to make.

Makes about 8 servings

3 large sweet red peppers
1 Tbsp olive oil or coconut oil
1 sweet onion, finely chopped
1 can (28 oz) diced tomatoes
1 can (14 oz) coconut milk
8 cups vegetable or chicken stock

1 Tbsp miso paste (optional)
1 tsp Dijon mustard (optional)
Salt and pepper to taste
Handful of fresh basil (optional, for a fancy garnish)

1. Preheat the broiler to high. Place the peppers in a baking dish then broil the peppers, turning often with tongs while wearing an oven mitt, until the peppers are charred on all sides.

2. Here comes the cool part: Place the peppers in a closed paper bag or in a covered glass dish until they are cool enough to handle, about 20 minutes. Peel the peppers and pull them apart, discarding the stems and seeds. Cut the roasted peppers into chunks, then set them aside for later.

3. In a large pot, heat the oil over medium-high heat. Add the onion and cook, stirring often, until it is softened, about 8 minutes. Add the broiled peppers to the pot and cook, stirring often, until heated through, about 5 minutes.

4. Add the tomatoes (with their juices), coconut milk, stock, and miso paste and mustard (if using). Bring to a boil over medium-high heat. Reduce the heat to medium-low and simmer, covered, for 10 minutes.

5. Take the lid off the soup and let cool for about 20 minutes. While you are waiting, think of all the people you want to invite over for dinner! Using an immersion blender in the pot, blend the soup until smooth (I love this part!). Season with salt and pepper to taste.

6. Reheat the soup over medium heat. Ladle the soup into warm bowls and sprinkle with a little bit of fresh basil if you really want to show off.

nana's potato soup

Lennox Douglas Kane Leaver
Age 10, Okotoks, AB

I like the soup because of the taste. Instead of milk I like to use the whey left over from when my nana makes cheese. Even my great-grandma made this soup.

Makes about 6 to 8 servings

2 to 3 Tbsp olive oil
4 to 6 stalks celery, chopped
1 medium onion, chopped
2 medium carrots, peeled and chopped
6 to 8 medium potatoes, peeled and chopped
4 cups vegetable stock
4 cups milk
Salt and pepper to taste

1. Heat the olive oil in a large pot. Add the celery and onion and cook, stirring often, until the onion starts to soften.

2. The chopped carrots go in next. Cook them, stirring often, for as long as you can—this is the key to good flavor.

3. Add the potatoes next, along with the stock and milk. Simmer until the potatoes are tender.

4. Season with salt and pepper to taste. Ladle the hearty soup into warm bowls.

cream of kohlrabi soup with smoked salmon

Michael Allemeier

Chef and Culinary Arts Instructor, SAIT, Calgary, AB

Kohlrabi is one of those unsung vegetable heroes. It is often overlooked in the grocery store or market and I find that sad, as it's very easy to prepare and can be enjoyed both raw and cooked. In its cooked form, it reminds me of broccoli stems. This gentle green flavor is perfect with seafood. Don't judge this vegetable's appearance; it's delicious!

Makes about 8 servings

⅓ cup butter
1 onion, chopped
1 small fennel bulb, cored and chopped
2 cloves garlic, sliced
2 medium kohlrabi root, peeled and finely chopped
12 cups vegetable or chicken stock
1 cup cream
Salt to taste
3 slices cold smoked salmon per person
½ cup chives, finely chopped

1. Melt the butter over medium heat and add the chopped onion and fennel, stirring often until tender but not colored, for about 6 to 8 minutes. Remember to stir often.

2. Add the sliced garlic and chopped kohlrabi and cook for about 1 to 2 minutes or until the garlic is fragrant.

3. Add the stock and bring to a simmer. Simmer for 20 minutes or until tender.

4. Add the cream and simmer for 10 more minutes.

5. Purée well and season with salt to taste.

6. Just before serving, place three slices of smoked salmon in each warmed bowl and pour soup over top of the salmon. Garnish soup with chopped chives.

See Michael's son's recipe on page 95!

attack of the killer tomatoes

Simon Drever
Age 12, Calgary, AB

My mom had this soup every Halloween when she was growing up. The recipe is dedicated to my sister, Edyn. She loved this soup with grilled cheese. I just like it on a cold day by itself. I love tomatoes but don't like soups with chunks so this one is smooth.

Makes about 8 servings

2 to 3 cans (each 28 oz) whole tomatoes (depends on how tomato-y you like it)
2 Tbsp olive oil
½ small onion, finely chopped
1 tsp granulated sugar
2 cloves garlic, minced
3 cups chicken or vegetable stock
½ cup packed fresh basil leaves, cut into thin strips
1 tsp salt
¼ tsp pepper
1½ cups whipping cream (35% MF; optional)

1. Open the cans of tomatoes and, with kitchen scissors, snip the tomatoes into smaller pieces right in the cans. Set the cans aside for later.

2. In a large pot, heat the oil over medium-low heat. Add the onion and sugar and cook, stirring often, until the onion has softened, about 8 minutes. Add the garlic and cook, stirring, until it smells good, about 30 seconds.

3. Add the canned tomatoes (with their juices), stock, basil, salt and pepper. Bring to a boil over medium-high heat. Reduce the heat to medium-low and simmer, uncovered, for 30 minutes.

4. Remove the pot from the heat. Using an immersion blender in the pot, blend the soup until smooth. Whisk in the cream (if using) and heat through over medium heat.

5. Ladle the soup into warm bowls and eat it with or without grilled cheese.

If you leave out the cream this soup can be suitable for vegans.

walla walla onion soup

Matthew, Connor, Austin and Charlotte Batey
Executive Chef, The Nash, and kids, ages 17, 12, and 6, Calgary, AB

My father, Ian, started the tradition of making French onion soup with Walla Walla onions when the sweet bulbs come into season in early summer, and now I continue the ritual. The soup combines the best local ingredients and, although made using a classic technique, it's very simple. Topped generously with melted cheese, it's no wonder our family loves it. Be sure to make enough to freeze some to enjoy during the winter.

Makes 6 servings

6 Tbsp grapeseed oil
¼ cup butter (approx.)
3 Walla Walla onions, thinly sliced (see sidebar)
3 cloves garlic, minced
1 sprig fresh rosemary
1 tsp fresh thyme leaves
½ tsp ground coriander
½ tsp ground fennel
½ tsp ground star anise
Pepper to taste
½ cup red wine (optional)
¼ cup sherry (optional)
8 cups beef or veal stock
¼ cup sherry vinegar
Salt to taste
6 Croûtes (recipe follows)
1¼ cups shredded aged firm cheese, such as Gruyère
3 Tbsp finely chopped parsley

1. In a large, wide pot, heat the oil and butter over medium heat. Add the onions and garlic and cook, stirring often, until the onions start to soften, about 8 minutes.

2. Stir in the rosemary, thyme, coriander, fennel, star anise and pepper to taste. Continue to cook the onions, stirring occasionally, as they now start to color,

Named for Walla Walla County in Washington State where it's grown, the Walla Walla onion is sweet and very juicy. Don't be surprised if the onions take a long time to brown, as their moisture needs to cook out first. If you can't find Walla Walla onions, any sweet onions can be used.

If you use vegetable stock instead of beef stock, this soup is suitable for vegetarians.

Be wary of letting small hands near the heat of the soup bowls. Let younger children help prepare the croûtes, then place each one on a bowl of soup to avoid burns on tender fingertips.

adding a little more butter if the onions start to stick to the bottom of the pot. Cook, stirring occasionally, until the onions are evenly browned but not burnt, about 20 minutes.

3. Add the red wine and sherry (if using) and let the liquid bubble as you stir to loosen any brown bits on the bottom of the pot.

4. Add the stock and bring to a boil over medium-high heat. Reduce the heat to medium-low and simmer, uncovered, until the soup tastes good, about 1 hour.

5. Fish out and discard the rosemary sprig. Stir in the sherry vinegar and season with salt to taste.

6. Preheat the broiler to high. Set six onion soup or other ovenproof bowls on a large rimmed baking sheet. Ladle the soup into the bowls. Top each portion with a croûte, then sprinkle evenly with cheese.

7. Place the baking sheet with the bowls about 4 inches from the broiler and broil until the cheese melts and is golden, about 5 minutes.

8. Carefully remove the baking sheet from the oven and let the soup stand for 5 minutes. Sprinkle parsley over each bowl—it really adds a refreshing flavor to the soup—then enjoy!

See Matthew's daughter's recipe on page 191!

croûtes

makes 6 croûtes

6 Tbsp bacon fat (see sidebar)
6 slices brioche bread, trimmed to fit the top of your soup bowls

1. In a large skillet, heat the bacon fat over medium heat.

2. Add the slices of brioche to the skillet and cook, turning once or twice, until the slices are golden and crisp, about 6 minutes. Remove the croûtes from the skillet and drain on a paper-towel-lined plate.

miso corn chowder with blistered peppers

Tara O'Brady
Cookbook Author and Blogger, *sevenspoons.net*

Since we live in a city surrounded by farmland, my two sons are more than used to our errands relocating from a grocery store to outdoor markets and roadside stands in the warmer months. The seasonal shift in routine has taught my kids to mark the months by what's in season—they know that strawberries will be here at the end of May with the rhubarb and asparagus, then cherries, beets, beans and peaches following, before we move into melons, tomatoes and corn. Where we are in southern Ontario, the winters can be harsh and long, and the boys (and I) tend to treat the summer's high days as feast ones, filling up on our favorites while the going is good. They both adore corn, and after we've had it boiled, roasted-in-husks and blackened bare, I start up with pickled corn salads, empanadas and cool bowls of gazpacho. Finally, as the nights get cooler, it's one last hurrah with a gutsy corn and miso chowder. Made with a quick corn stock and bulked up with potatoes and squash, the soup eases us into the fall with miso's rounded, deep saltiness and an overall feeling of substance, yet still the soup is kept kicky with the smolder of roasted peppers and a dash of cold cream.

Depending on the brand, miso can vary wildly—some will be mild, others pungent and quite salty—so it is best to taste as you go and adjust the measurement accordingly.

Makes about 4 to 6 servings

4 ears corn, husked
3 cloves garlic, peeled and crushed with the flat side of a large knife
2 leeks, trimmed and outer leaves removed
6 cups water
1 tsp salt
3 Tbsp butter
6 oz fingerling or small potatoes, scrubbed and finely chopped

1 lb yellow summer squash (about 1 large), trimmed and finely chopped
1 small fresh red chili, stemmed and minced
1 to 2 Tbsp white (shiro) miso
¼ cup whipping cream (35% MF), plus more to serve
Pepper to taste
Blistered padrón peppers, finely chopped (see sidebar on next page)

1. Snap each of the ears of corn in half. Stand one piece up on its flat end on a rimmed baking sheet, then cut the kernels off with a sturdy knife. Repeat with the remaining pieces until all are stripped. Set the corn kernels aside and put the ears in a large pot along with the garlic cloves.

Padrón peppers look like shriveled jalapeños; look for them in specialty produce stores or larger supermarkets. Some can be quite spicy while others have no heat at all. So, if serving to small children, taste them before adding to the soup.

For this recipe, you will need 6 oz of peppers. Wash and dry them well. Then, heat 1 Tbsp of unroasted sesame oil in a large skillet over medium-high heat until shimmering and starting to smoke.

Standing back, tumble in the peppers. Cook, tossing often, until they are blistered and charred on all sides, 3 to 5 minutes.

Then, tip them into a bowl, season with flaky sea salt and serve at once. You can eat these whole as a snack or appetizer, or chop them finely for garnish.

2. Trim the dark green ends of the leeks from the pale green and white ends. Split the dark green pieces lengthwise and wash them under cold running water to remove any grit. Add the dark green pieces to the pot with the ears of corn. Finely chop the pale green and white parts of the leeks, then put them in a bowl of cold water and set aside to soak.

3. Add the water and salt to the pot and bring to a boil over high heat. Reduce heat to medium-low and simmer, partially covered, for 30 minutes.

4. Meanwhile, melt the butter in a second large pot over medium heat. Add the potatoes and cook, stirring often, for 3 minutes.

5. Drain the finely chopped leeks and add them to the potatoes (don't worry about draining them thoroughly—damp is fine). Add the squash and a confident pinch of salt. Cook, stirring often, until the vegetables are tender but without much color, 8 to 10 minutes. Stir in the minced chili and reserved corn kernels.

6. Strain the corn-ear stock through a fine-mesh sieve set over a large pitcher. Whisk 1 Tbsp of miso into the hot stock until it dissolves. Taste and check for seasoning; it should be salty. Add more miso if needed. Add the stock to the pot containing the vegetable mixture. Simmer, uncovered, for 5 minutes. (This is a good time to prep the padrón peppers.)

7. Remove the pot from the heat. Using an immersion blender in the pot, blend the soup until it is halfway smooth. Stir in the cream, then season with salt and pepper to taste. If the soup is too thick, add a little extra water or cream. Reheat the soup over medium heat if necessary.

8. Ladle the soup into warm bowls and add a drizzle of cream and some finely chopped blistered Padrón peppers.

charred tomato soup

John Jackson and Connie DeSousa
Chefs and Owners, Charcut Roast House, Calgary, AB

The best-tasting tomatoes, onions, carrots and basil will be those that you pick from your own garden.

Makes about 4 servings

6 vine-ripened tomatoes
1 Tbsp olive oil
1 Tbsp butter
1 onion, finely chopped
1 carrot, peeled and finely chopped
1 clove garlic, minced
3 cups chicken or vegetable stock

1 Tbsp tomato paste
12 fresh basil leaves
1 tsp salt
¼ tsp pepper
1 cup whipping cream (35% MF)
Fresh basil leaves for garnish

1. Preheat the broiler to high. Arrange the tomatoes in a single layer on a large rimmed baking sheet. Broil about 4 inches from the heat until the tomatoes begin to blister and char. Rotate the baking sheet and turn the tomatoes halfway through cooking so all sides have nice charred blisters, about 15 minutes. Set aside to cool.

2. In a large pot, heat the olive oil and butter over medium heat. Add the onion and carrots and cook, stirring often, until the onion has softened, about 7 minutes. Add the garlic and cook, stirring, for 1 minute.

3. Stir in the charred tomatoes, stock, tomato paste, basil, salt and pepper. Increase the heat to medium-high and bring the soup to a boil. Reduce the heat to medium-low and simmer, uncovered, until all the vegetables are very tender, 25 to 30 minutes.

4. Remove the pot from the heat. Using an immersion blender in the pot, blend the soup until smooth. Stir in the whipping cream and season with more salt and pepper to taste.

5. Bring the soup back to a simmer over medium heat, then ladle into warm bowls and serve with a scattering of whole or chopped fresh basil and crusty bread on the side, if you like.

creamy and bacony asparagus soup with dill croutons

Abby Major
Age 12, MasterChef Junior Semi-Finalist, Winchester, VA

I love this soup because it is creamy and bacony. It is inspired by the asparagus soup I made when I was a contestant on *MasterChef Junior*, but this has a lot more ingredients!

Makes about 6 servings

6 slices bacon, chopped, or ¼ cup chopped pancetta
1 tsp butter
1 medium onion, chopped
2 lb asparagus (about 2 bunches), tough ends snapped off
6 cups chicken stock
Salt and pepper to taste
2 Tbsp crème fraîche or plain Greek yogurt
Dill Croutons (recipe opposite)

1. In a large pot over medium-low heat, fry the bacon, stirring often, until crispy, about 5 minutes. Use a slotted spoon to remove the bacon from the pot but not the bacon fat. Put the bacon in a bowl and set aside for later.

2. Add the butter to the bacon fat and melt over low heat. Add the onion and cook, stirring often, until the onion has softened, about 8 minutes.

3. Meanwhile, coarsely chop the asparagus. Add the asparagus to the pot, along with the chicken stock and salt and pepper to taste. Bring to a boil over medium-high heat. Reduce the heat to low and simmer, covered, until the asparagus is very tender, about 20 minutes.

4. Remove the pot from the heat and add the crème fraîche. Using an immersion blender in the pot, blend the soup until smooth.

5. Ladle the soup into warm bowls and sprinkle with the reserved crispy bacon and dill croutons (recipe opposite).

dill croutons

¼ cup butter
½ loaf of any style artisanal bread, cut into 1-inch cubes
2 tsp chopped fresh dill
Salt and pepper to taste

1. In a large skillet, melt the butter over medium-low heat. Add the bread cubes and gently toss to coat in the butter. Cook, stirring often, until the bread is browned and crispy, 5 to 7 minutes.

2. Remove from the heat, then sprinkle the croutons with dill and salt and pepper to taste.

If you omit the bacon and substitute vegetable stock for the chicken stock, this can be a vegetarian dish. Omit the croutons and it's suitable for anyone on a gluten-free diet.

Add more crème fraîche if you want a creamier soup. Also, you can try different seasonings on the croutons for a different taste. Enjoy!

tortilla soup

Earls Restaurants

Looking for a recipe that can be customized to individual tastes? This is the perfect candidate. It is healthy, filling and can be garnished accordingly. Kids will love preparing the vegetables and shredding cheese alongside you, and nothing beats giving them the "power of choice" to encourage empty bowls in the end. See the sidebar for additional garnish ideas.

Makes about 4 servings

Pasilla chilies can be found in Mexican or specialty grocery stores, or the produce section of some large supermarkets.

This soup is gluten free as long as the corn tortillas are made in a gluten-free facility.

Corn kernels, drained, canned black beans, finely chopped cilantro, or diced tomato or sweet pepper can also be added as garnishes.

soup
2 Tbsp canola or corn oil, divided
¼ cup finely chopped shallot
1 lb Roma tomatoes, cored and cut in half lengthwise
⅔ cup canned crushed tomatoes
½ cup finely chopped onion
2 tsp minced garlic
4 cups vegetable stock
1 Tbsp finely chopped fresh oregano leaves
2½ tsp salt
¼ tsp black pepper

garnish
Two 6-inch yellow, red or blue corn tortillas
1 dried pasilla chili (optional; see sidebar)
Canola or corn oil for deep-frying
¼ tsp salt
1 avocado
¼ cup sour cream
¼ cup Mexican-blend shredded cheese
Hot sauce or chili oil (optional)

1. For the soup, heat 1 tsp oil in a large heavy-bottomed pot or Dutch oven over medium-high heat. Add the shallot and cook until translucent and fragrant, about 1 minute. Transfer to a medium bowl. Set the pot aside but do not wash.

2. To the bowl with the shallot, add the Roma tomatoes, crushed tomatoes, onion and garlic. Using an immersion blender in the bowl, blend the mixture until smooth.

3. In the same pot, heat the remaining oil over medium-high heat. Add the blended tomato mixture and bring to a slow simmer. Cook for 8 minutes, stirring occasionally.

4. Add the stock, oregano, salt and pepper. Return to a simmer, then remove the pot from the heat.

5. For the garnish, cut the tortillas in half, then cut each half into 2- x ⅛-inch strips.

6. Wearing gloves (chilies can irritate sensitive skin), remove the stem from the dried chili and cut the chili in half lengthwise. Remove and discard all the seeds. Slice the chili into 2- x ⅛-inch strips and set aside.

7. Pour the oil into a 2-quart saucepan to a depth of 2½ to 3 inches. Heat to 350°F over medium-high heat (check the temperature with a candy thermometer). Using a slotted spoon or a sieve, lower the tortilla strips into the oil and fry until crisp, about 45 seconds. Remove with the slotted spoon and drain immediately on a paper-towel-lined plate. Season with salt.

8. Using the same slotted spoon or sieve, lower the chili strips into the oil and fry for 5 seconds. Remove with the slotted spoon and drain immediately on the paper-towel-lined plate, then pat dry with more paper towel.

9. Peel and pit the avocado, then cut it lengthwise into ¼-inch slices.

10. To serve, reheat the soup if necessary, then ladle into warm bowls. Garnish each serving with sliced avocado, a spoonful of sour cream, some shredded cheese, and a scattering of fried tortilla strips and chili (if using). Drizzle with hot sauce or chili oil, if you like.

roman "egg drop" soup

Lidia Matticchio Bastianich

Cookbook Author, TV Personality and Owner of Felidia, and three other restaurants, New York City, NY

Stracciare means "to rip to shreds" in Italian, and, indeed, that is how this soup looks after stirring beaten eggs with some grated cheese in a good chicken stock. Once you have a flavorful chicken stock, the rest is easy. Stracciatella is usually served with shredded spinach and beaten egg, but I recall having it with just egg and cheese when spinach was not in season. In the Italy that I grew up in, seasons made a difference—not only in how we dressed but in what we ate. This is a great restorative soup, served in most Italian homes.

Makes about 6 servings

8 cups chicken stock (preferably homemade; see page 15)
4 cups packed spinach leaves, shredded
1¼ tsp salt, divided
4 large eggs
⅓ cup freshly grated Grana Padano cheese, plus more for serving
Pepper to taste

1. In a medium pot, bring the stock to a simmer over medium heat. Once it is simmering, add the spinach and 1 tsp salt and cook until tender, about 3 minutes.

2. Meanwhile, whisk the eggs, grated cheese, the remaining salt and pepper to taste in a medium bowl.

3. Once the spinach is tender, start to whisk the spinach mixture and, whisking constantly, add about one-third of the egg mixture to the soup to make shreds of the eggs.

4. Bring the soup back to a simmer and whisk in half of the remaining egg mixture. Then, bring the soup back to a simmer again and whisk in the remaining egg mixture.

5. Once all of the egg mixture has been added, bring the soup to a final boil, whisking to break up any large clusters of egg.

6. Ladle the soup into warm bowls and serve at once with additional grated cheese.

This recipe is adapted from Lidia's Mastering the Art of Italian Cuisine *(Appetite by Random House, 2015).*

easy peasy carrot soup

Ricardo Larrivée
Food Writer and TV Personality

Making soup is just like math. And not even hard math, just simple addition. Easy peasy! Because it's such a breeze, you can change up the veggies, depending on what you like. Not keen on carrots? Use 6 cups of cauliflower or broccoli florets instead. Once you've nailed the basic recipe, feel free to add more vegetables (or not) to the recipe and make it your own. (P.S. chocolate is not a vegetable.) The result? Super soups that the whole family will love and that you invented on your own!

Makes about 4 servings

5 cups vegetable or chicken broth
4 cups peeled, chopped carrots
1 onion, chopped
Salt and pepper to taste

1. In a large saucepan, combine the broth, carrots and onion. Season with salt and pepper to taste.

2. Bring to a boil over medium-high heat. Reduce the heat to medium and simmer, uncovered, until the vegetables are very tender, about 30 minutes. The cooking time will vary depending on the vegetables you use.

3. Remove the pot from the heat. Using an immersion blender in the pot, blend the soup until smooth. Beware of splattering! Season with salt and pepper to taste.

4. Ladle the soup into warm bowls and feel very proud.

magic beans

FARMERS WORK HARD ON THEIR LAND TO PLANT SEEDS AND WATCH the fields fill with a blanket of green as lentils and beans and other crops begin to grow. These little seedlings thrive under the farmers' care and grow into bountiful plants heavy with split peas, chickpeas, beans and more. Even peanuts are actually part of the pulse family. Once harvested, this bounty appears in our local stores. Whether fresh, dried or canned, with these ingredients in hand, we have hearty fixings for all kinds of soups. In this chapter, you'll find soups filled with these pulses, like a minestrone speckled with chickpeas, a lentil soup with lots of warming spices from Morocco and a hearty peanut soup with a bit of a kick.

Bella Ribollita (page 97)

throw-it-all-in-the-pot pea soup

Eric Akis
Cookbook Author and Food Writer

My late French Canadian mother loved making hearty, no-fuss soups like this one. In fact, pea soup is a metaphor for who she was. Like her, it's humble, welcoming, heartwarming and sturdy, and I like to think she passed those qualities on to me. I guess that's why, when asked to contribute a recipe for this book, it was the first one I thought of. Make a meal of the soup by serving it with thick slices of buttered crusty bread.

Makes about 6 to 8 servings

1½ cups green or yellow split peas (see sidebar)	½ cup grated carrot
9 cups chicken or vegetable stock	½ tsp ground sage
5 oz sliced deli ham, such as country or black forest, chopped	½ tsp dried thyme leaves
1 cup finely chopped celery	½ tsp dried marjoram leaves
1 cup finely chopped onion	⅛ tsp cayenne
	Salt and pepper to taste
	2 green onions, thinly sliced (optional)

1. Rinse the peas well in cold water, then drain well.

2. Put the peas in a large pot, along with the stock, ham, celery, onion, carrot, sage, thyme, marjoram and cayenne. Bring the soup to a gentle simmer over medium-high heat (small bubbles should just break on the surface).

3. Reduce the heat to medium-low to maintain that gentle simmer, then simmer the soup, partially covered, until peas are very tender and the soup has thickened, 50 to 60 minutes. (Add a little more stock or water if the soup has reduced too much and become too thick.)

4. Season the soup with salt and pepper to taste, and that's all there is to it. Ladle the soup into warm bowls, scatter with green onions (if using) and dive in.

Handling Split Peas

A split pea is a skinned, dried pea divided in two. Because they're split, liquid can more easily penetrate the peas, which is why they don't need to be soaked in water before cooking like other pulses, such as dried beans. Store them in a tightly sealed container in a cool, dark, dry place and use them within a year of purchasing. The longer they are stored, the drier the peas become, which, in turn, increases cooking time. If they take forever to cook, they are past their prime and it's time to get new ones.

20-minute chickpea-spinach stew

Karlynn Johnston
Cookbook Author and Blogger, thekitchenmagpie.com

It's hard to believe something so fast and simple can taste so good. This stew is packed with protein, vegetables and flavor—everything a busy family on the go needs. The secret to creating a great-tasting tomato-based soup is to add a tiny sprinkle of granulated sugar, which cuts the acidity, making it less harsh on children's developing palates. Have you ever wondered why kids love ketchup so much? It's the sugar. And a little bit will go a long way in this soup.

Makes about 4 servings

1 Tbsp olive oil
½ cup chopped red onion
3 cloves garlic, minced
1 can (28 oz) diced tomatoes
¼ tsp granulated sugar, or more to taste
2 tsp instant vegetable stock powder
1 can (19 oz) chickpeas, drained and rinsed
6 cups lightly packed baby spinach leaves

1. In a large pot, heat the oil over medium heat. Add the onion and cook, stirring often, until the onion has softened, about 8 minutes. Add the garlic and cook, stirring, until it smells good, about 1 minute.

2. Add the tomatoes (with their juices), sugar and vegetable stock powder and stir until the sugar and stock powder have dissolved.

3. Add the chickpeas, then bring to a low boil over medium-high heat. Reduce the heat to medium-low and simmer, uncovered and stirring occasionally, until the flavors have developed to your liking, 5 to 10 minutes.

4. Stir in the spinach and simmer until it has wilted, about 2 minutes. Ladle the soup into warm bowls and dig in.

This recipe can be easily adapted to suit your family's tastes:

- Switch out the chickpeas for white beans and add some dried Italian herb seasoning for a taste of Italy.

- Add a little cooked ground chicken or turkey for a meatier version.

- Use dried beans instead of canned (follow the instructions on page 8 for cooking with dried beans).

lotsa vegetables soup with lentils

Anjali Pathak
Chef, Food Writer and Founder of Flavour Diaries, Mumbai, India

Soups are the ultimate comfort food. I've made this dish hundreds of times and it never fails to hit the spot. You can use any vegetables you like, but I'm going for carrots, broccoli and spinach and using lentils to add some body to it.

Makes about 4 servings

1½ cups dried green or brown lentils, rinsed and drained
3 Tbsp canola or light olive oil, divided
2 onions, thinly sliced
1 tsp cumin seeds
2 bay leaves
3 carrots, finely chopped
2 stalks celery, finely chopped
2 cloves garlic, finely chopped
1 Tbsp garam masala (see page 34)
6½ cups vegetable stock
2 cups broccoli florets or baby broccoli
2 handfuls of spinach leaves
Juice of ½ lemon, or to taste
Salt and pepper to taste
Roasted or fresh chilies for garnish (optional, see sidebar)

For a spicy kick, feel free to add roasted or fresh chilies to this soup, as pictured.

1. Put the lentils in a medium bowl and add enough cold water to cover them. Set aside to soak for 30 minutes, then drain well and set aside for later.

2. Meanwhile, heat 2 Tbsp of the oil in a large pot over medium heat. Add the onions and cook, stirring often, until they are light golden brown, about 10 minutes. Take half of the onions out of the pot and set them aside for later. Continue cooking the onions in the pot, stirring often, until they are deep golden brown and crispy, about 5 more minutes. Take these onions out of the pot and set aside separate from the first onions (you'll use these crispy onions for garnishing the soup later).

3. Heat the remaining oil in the pot over medium heat. Add the cumin and bay

This soup can be garnished with a dollop of yogurt at the end, if you like.

leaves. Add back the softened onions (that's the first batch you took out of the pot), along with the lentils, carrots, celery, garlic and garam masala.

4. Add the stock and bring the soup to a boil over medium-high heat. Reduce heat to medium-low and simmer, uncovered, until the lentils and vegetables are tender, about 40 minutes.

5. Remove the pot from the heat. Fish out and discard the bay leaves. Using an immersion blender in the pot, blitz the soup a few times (I like to leave some texture).

6. Bring the soup to a simmer and add the broccoli. Cook, uncovered, for 2 minutes. Add the spinach and turn off the heat. Season the soup with lemon juice, salt and pepper to taste.

7. Ladle the soup into warm bowls and serve each portion topped with the reserved crispy onions and some roasted or fresh chilies, if you like.

This recipe is adapted from The Indian Family Kitchen *(Appetite by Random House, 2016).*

lachlan's classic minestrone

Lachlan Allemeier
Age 13, Calgary, AB

I made this soup with a little help from my dad (his recipe is on page 70), and then shared it on CBC when he was on the radio. I liked being on the radio.

Makes about 8 servings

¼ cup olive oil

3 shallots, thinly sliced

2 leeks (white parts only), thinly sliced

2 cloves garlic, coarsely chopped

1 cup peeled and finely chopped yams

1 cup peeled and finely chopped potatoes

1 cup peeled and finely chopped carrots

1 cup peeled and finely chopped parsnips

2 cups ½-inch sliced garlic sausage

6 cups chicken stock

2 cups cherry tomatoes, cut in half

1 cup cooked and drained canned white beans

5 sprigs fresh thyme

2 bay leaves

1 cup fresh or frozen peas

½ cup coarsely chopped parsley

Salt to taste

Pinch of red chili flakes

1. In a large pot, heat the oil over medium heat. Add the shallots, leeks and garlic and cook, stirring often, until they are softened, about 8 minutes.

2. Add the yams, potatoes, carrots, parsnips and garlic sausage and stir well. Cook, stirring occasionally, until the carrots start to soften at the edges, about 5 minutes.

3. Add the stock, tomatoes, beans, thyme and bay leaves, then bring the soup to a simmer over medium-high heat. Reduce the heat to medium-low and simmer, uncovered, until all the vegetables are tender, about 10 minutes.

4. Add the peas and parsley and bring the soup back to a simmer. Fish out and discard the thyme and bay leaves, then season with salt to taste and a pinch of red chili flakes.

5. Ladle the soup into warm bowls and enjoy. (Yes, you have to—it's so yummy!)

bella ribollita

Debbie Travis
TV Personality and Lifestyle Guru

Several years ago, I fell madly in love with a run-down villa in Tuscany, the Italian people and the food. I bought the property, renovated it and started a Girls' Getaway where women could stay and spend a week with me detoxing their minds and bodies under the Tuscan sun. It has changed my life. The meals are one of the highlights at Villa Reniella. The vegetables are picked daily from our organic *orto* or veggie garden, and all the other ingredients come from local farms. We are lucky to have a passionate and brilliant chef, Francesco, who creates the most delicious lunches and dinners for our groups of women. Tuscany was originally a poor farming region and the Tuscans used cooking techniques that gleaned the most nutrition from whatever seasonal ingredients could be found. These traditions have carried on into every home kitchen and restaurant. Francesco shares some of these recipes with us during his lively cooking classes. One of his and all the guests' favorites is Ribollita. This is a rustic Italian peasant dish that is incredibly tasty, and even more so the next day. When reheated, the flavors really intensify.

A bowl of steaming, hot soup is packed with memories. I was brought up in the north of England where every spare minute was spent outside, rain or shine but mostly rain. We would be summoned inside at "tea time," usually for a mug of homemade soup. Always homemade, my mum would use any leftovers to cook the yummiest, chunky vegetable soup. There was always some kind of stock on the boil in our house, made from peelings and chicken bones. In that childhood kitchen, I learned the wonders of soup—fast, cheap, nutritious and hearty.

Makes 8 servings

¼ cup olive oil
2 stalks celery, finely chopped
1 onion, finely chopped
1 carrot, peeled and finely chopped
1 potato, peeled and finely chopped
2 zucchini, peeled, seeded and finely chopped
4 cups vegetable stock
Salt to taste
1 bunch cavolo nero, kale or chard, stems removed and leaves shredded

½ savoy cabbage, cored and shredded
2 cups drained and rinsed canned cannellini beans
8 slices Tuscan or other rustic bread
¼ cup finely chopped parsley
¼ cup finely chopped fresh basil
Pepper to taste
Freshly grated Pecorino Romano cheese (optional)
Paprika (optional)

1. In a large skillet, heat the oil over medium heat. Add the celery, onion and carrot. Cook, stirring occasionally, until the onion is starting to soften, about 4 minutes. Add the potato and zucchini and stir to coat with the onion mixture.

Years later, when my career exploded in Canada, our Sundays were often spent making a variety of soups that would take the family through the week. Today, I love to watch my grown lads create their own fancy versions of my soups. The soup memories keep on going through the generations.

If you prefer, use 1½ cups dried cannellini beans, instead of the canned beans, following the soaking and cooking instructions on page 8.

2. Gradually stir in the stock, little by little, as if you were cooking a risotto. Add 3 big pinches of salt and bring it all to a boil over medium-high heat. Reduce the heat to medium-low and simmer, uncovered, for 40 minutes.

3. Add the cavolo nero and savoy cabbage to the pot, then stir in the beans. Simmer the soup for 20 more minutes.

4. For a truly traditional presentation, preheat the oven to 350°F. Put eight bowls on a large rimmed baking sheet. Just before serving the soup, toast the bread until golden on both sides and put one slice in each of the bowls. At the last moment, in order to preserve their aromatic flavor, add the parsley, basil and pepper to taste to the soup.

5. Ladle the soup over the toasted bread in the bowls. Sprinkle each serving with cheese, if you like. Put the baking sheet with the bowls in the oven until the cheese has melted, about 3 minutes.

6. For a simpler presentation, just ladle the soup over the toasted bread in the bowls and sprinkle each serving with a little paprika (if using). Serve at once.

zesty peanut soup

Gwendolyn Richards

Food Writer, Cookbook Author and Blogger, patentandthepantry.com

Who says peanut butter only belongs in sandwiches? Sure, we often think of jelly or jam as peanut butter's best friend, but mixing it with tomatoes makes a creamy, warming soup that's full of unexpected flavor. The soup is rich, but the lime juice and a hint of spice from hot pepper sauce—which can be omitted for kids who don't like that little kick—round it out perfectly.

Makes about 4 servings

2 Tbsp vegetable oil
1 small onion, finely chopped
½ tsp salt, divided
3 cloves garlic, minced
1 tsp minced fresh ginger
2 Tbsp tomato paste
1 can (28 oz) diced tomatoes
3 cups vegetable or chicken stock
1 cup smooth peanut butter

½ cup roasted peanuts, coarsely chopped, plus more for garnish
3 green onions, thinly sliced
1 Tbsp hot pepper sauce, plus more for serving
¼ tsp pepper
Juice of 2 limes
Lime wedges for garnish

1. In a large pot, heat the oil over medium heat. Add the onion and half of the salt and cook, stirring often, until the onion is soft and translucent, about 5 minutes.

2. Add the garlic and ginger and cook, stirring, for about 1 minute, until it smells good. Stir in the tomato paste and cook, stirring, for 1 minute.

3. Add the tomatoes (with their juices) and stock. Increase the heat to medium-high and bring to a simmer. Add the peanut butter and stir thoroughly until the peanut butter melts into the soup. Reduce the heat to medium-low, cover the pot and simmer for about 15 minutes.

4. Add the peanuts, green onions, hot pepper sauce, the rest of the salt and the pepper. Add most of the lime juice, then carefully taste the soup. If it is still a bit rich or bland, add the rest of the lime juice and a bit more hot pepper sauce, if you like.

5. Ladle the soup into warm bowls and serve with lime wedges for squeezing and hot pepper sauce for shaking.

This recipe is adapted from Pucker: A Cookbook for Citrus Lovers *(Whitecap Books, 2014).*

indian comfort-food soup

Vikram Vij
Cookbook Author and Chef and Owner, Vij's, Vancouver, BC, and three other restaurants

The Indian name for this soup is *rajma chawal*. It's sometimes called "Indian mac and cheese," not because it contains macaroni or cheese, but because it's value-for-money comfort food, and a favorite with kids (including mine!), students and families. The beans provide low-fat protein, and the spices add wonderful flavor.

Makes about 6 servings

½ cup vegetable oil
2 cups chopped onion (about 1 large)
2 Tbsp minced garlic (about 6 medium cloves)
1½ cups chopped tomatoes (about 3 medium)
2 Tbsp minced fresh ginger
1½ Tbsp chili powder
1 Tbsp ground cumin
1 Tbsp ground coriander

1½ tsp salt
1 tsp ground turmeric
1 tsp pepper (optional)
1 tsp cayenne (optional)
½ cup plain yogurt, stirred (optional)
5 to 6 cups water (see sidebar)
3 cans (each 14 oz) kidney beans, drained and rinsed
5 to 6 cups cooked white or brown basmati rice

Curry is like a hearty soup that can be thicker or thinner depending on how much water you add. Like a soupier soup? Add the full 6 cups of water or even more to get the consistency you like.

If you choose not to add yogurt, this recipe will be vegan.

1. In a medium saucepan, heat the oil over medium-high heat for about 30 seconds. Add the onion and cook, stirring often, until it is slightly dark brown, about 8 minutes.

2. Add the garlic and cook, stirring, until it smells good, about 2 minutes. Stir in the tomatoes and ginger.

3. Add the chili powder, cumin, coriander, salt, turmeric and pepper and cayenne (if using). This is called a masala. Cook the masala, stirring often, until oil glistens on top, 5 to 8 minutes.

4. Place the yogurt (if using) in a small bowl. To prevent curdling, spoon about 2 Tbsp of the hot masala into the yogurt. Stir well, then pour the yogurt into the pot of masala. Cook, stirring, until the oil glistens on top again, about 2 minutes.

5. Stir in the water and bring to a boil over high heat. Add the kidney beans, stir well and bring to a boil again. Reduce the heat to medium and cook for 3 minutes.

6. Pour the soup into a large serving bowl and serve alongside the rice so everyone can help themselves buffet-style.

"french canadian" pea soup

Karen Miller
Soup Sister

I watched my mother make this soup often. She was Norwegian, not French Canadian, but we lived in Quebec. Norwegians also love to make pea soup and this is her version of a Canadian classic.

Hearty and healthy, it was my son's favorite soup for lunch or dinner when he was growing up. This is a great soup to get kids cooking: a little chopping, a little cooking, a little simmering and a little stirring and that's it! The soup offers simple flavors that can easily be adjusted to any taste buds.

Makes about 4 servings

2 Tbsp butter or vegetable oil
2 carrots, peeled and finely chopped
1 onion, peeled and finely chopped
1 stalk celery with leaves, finely chopped
8 cups water
1 lb dried yellow or green split peas, rinsed and drained
1 piece of ham bone or 1 chunk of boneless ham
1 bay leaf
Salt and pepper to taste
Chopped fresh parsley for garnish (optional)

1. In a large pot, melt the butter over medium heat. Add the carrots, onion and celery and cook, stirring often, until the onion starts to soften, about 5 minutes.

2. Add the water, split peas, ham bone or ham chunk and bay leaf. Add a little more water, if necessary, so all the ingredients are covered. Bring to a boil over medium-high heat.

3. Reduce the heat to low and simmer, uncovered, until the peas start to break down, about 1 hour, or until the soup reaches the desired consistency.

4. Fish out and discard the ham bone and bay leaf. If using a chunk of ham, chop the ham and return it to the soup. Season with salt and pepper to taste. Ladle the soup into warm bowls and scatter with parsley (if using).

This soup can be made in a slow cooker if you prefer. Follow the recipe through step 2 then pour into a slow cooker and cook on low for 6 to 8 hours until the soup reaches the desired consistency.

This soup freezes well but will thicken on cooling so you may want to add more water when you reheat the soup.

If you omit the ham and use vegetable oil instead of butter, this soup is suitable for vegetarians or vegans.

middle eastern minestrone

Nigella Lawson
Cookbook Author and Television Personality

This is in no sense an authentically Middle Eastern recipe, but a fancy of mine. To elucidate: it is a vegetable soup that is imbued with Middle Eastern flavors and, in place of the pasta that you'd find in a traditional Italian minestrone, I use bulgur wheat.

Like many such soups, it thickens on standing, in which case you can either add more liquid, or eat it as a stew. Either way, it is fragrant and filling, and is fast becoming one of my favorite recipes.

Makes about 6 servings

Preserved lemons are a condiment used in North African cooking made by preserving whole lemons in brine. They're tart and very lemony and add a unique flavor to stews and soups. Look for them in specialty grocery stores.

2 Tbsp olive oil
1 red onion, chopped
Salt to taste
1 butternut squash, peeled, seeded and cut into 1-inch cubes
1 clove garlic, minced
2 tsp cumin seeds
2 tsp coriander seeds

2 to 3 preserved lemons (depending on the size), finely chopped (see sidebar)
1½ cups chickpeas, cooked or drained from a can
6 cups vegetable stock
⅔ cup bulgur wheat
Roughly chopped cilantro for garnish (optional)

1. In a large pot that comes with a lid, heat the olive oil over medium heat. Add the onion and sprinkle with a little salt, then cook, stirring often, until the onion is starting to soften, about 3 minutes.

2. Add the butternut squash, garlic, and cumin and coriander seeds. Stir everything around and let it cook, stirring occasionally, for about 10 minutes.

3. Tip in the preserved lemons and chickpeas, then pour in the vegetable stock and partially cover the pot with the lid to keep the liquid from evaporating too much. Simmer for about 20 minutes, by which time the butternut squash should be just cooked.

4. Add the bulgur wheat, then cook gently, partially covered, for 10 more minutes, by which time the vegetables should be tender and the bulgur wheat soft but still nutty.

5. Ladle the soup into warm bowls and serve sprinkled with chopped cilantro (if using).

This recipe is adapted from Simply Nigella *(Appetite by Random House, 2015).*

pea soup with crème fraîche and crispy bacon chips

Zac Kara
Age 14, *MasterChef Junior* Participant, YouTuber, youtube.com/c/zackara, Orlando, FL

This is an easy and delicious soup that is incredibly healthy. Peas are a good source of protein.

Makes about 2 servings

2 green onions, cut into thirds
4 cups fresh or frozen peas
1 cup milk
½ to ¾ cup whipping cream (35% MF)
Salt and pepper to taste
2 Tbsp crème fraîche for garnish
Bacon Chips (recipe follows)
Crackers for serving

1. Fill a large saucepan with water and bring it to a boil. Fill a large bowl with cold water and ice.

2. Add the green onions to the saucepan of boiling water and cook for 45 seconds (this is called blanching). Using a slotted spoon, remove the green onions from the boiling water and immediately put them in the bowl of ice water.

3. Add the peas to the saucepan of boiling water and blanch them until they are soft, about 3 minutes for fresh peas and 1 minute for frozen. Using the slotted spoon, remove all the peas from the boiling water and add them to the green onions in the bowl of ice water.

4. Set a large colander in the sink and drain the bowl of peas and green onions through the colander. Discard any remaining ice. Tip the pea mixture back into the bowl.

5. Add the milk, ½ cup whipping cream and salt and pepper to taste to the pea mixture. In a blender, blend the soup until smooth. If the soup is too thick, blend in the remaining cream. Pour the soup into a pot and heat gently over medium heat to serve.

6. Ladle the soup into warm bowls, top each serving with a dollop of crème fraîche, then garnish with bacon chips (recipe follows) and serve with crackers.

bacon chips

2 slices bacon (see sidebar)
2 tsp grapeseed oil

If you like, you can use turkey bacon instead.

1. Using a very small cookie cutter, cut the bacon slices into rounds, or chop them coarsely.

2. In a small nonstick skillet, heat the oil over medium heat. Add the bacon and cook, stirring often, until very crisp, 5 to 7 minutes.

3. Using a slotted spoon, remove the bacon chips from the skillet and drain on a paper-towel-lined plate.

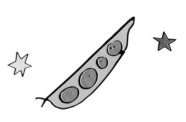

armenian lentil and rice soup

Tony Minichiello
Chef and Co-owner, Northwest Culinary Academy, Vancouver, BC

This has been my family's go-to soup not only on rainy, gray days, but when the spirit simply needs some comforting. No heirloom dish made the kids happier, which led me to believe they were perhaps more Armenian (my wife's heritage) than Italian (mine). We ate this as a meal—two bowls each—with bread. Very humbling, but it did the job. The main thing is how simple the recipe actually is, and adding to it (as I tried on a couple of occasions) did not help but hurt the emotional value of this fine soup. Now that my boys have moved on, it is only appropriate the soup warms up the soul of other families.

Makes about 4 servings

6 cups water
1 cup red lentils, rinsed and drained
2 Tbsp basmati rice, rinsed and drained
1 tsp salt
⅓ cup olive oil
1 medium onion, finely chopped
Lemon wedges
Cayenne pepper, ground cumin, chopped parsley and/or pepper to taste

1. In a large pot, combine the water, lentils, rice and salt. Cover and bring to a simmer over medium heat. Cook until the lentils disintegrate and rice swells up, at least 30 minutes (you can't overcook this one).

2. Meanwhile, in a small skillet, heat the oil over medium-low heat. Add the onion and cook, stirring occasionally, until it is very lightly browned, about 10 minutes.

3. Adjust the consistency of the soup if necessary by adding a little more water to thin it down. Our family prefers it as a thin porridge, something that pours like cream, rather than something thick that sticks to your spoon. Taste and add more salt if necessary.

4. Pour the contents of the skillet into the soup, being careful to add all of the olive oil.

5. Ladle the soup into warm bowls and add a squeeze of fresh lemon juice to each serving. Let everyone season their own soup with their choice of cayenne pepper, cumin, parsley and/or pepper.

The key to this simple recipe is the layers. Trying to make it all in one pot, and with chicken stock rather than water (as I once tried to do thinking I could do better than my wife) takes away from the simple wisdom of this soup. It is, after all, a hand-me-down recipe. I used to add cumin to mine at the table, but my sons have never followed my lead. I now eat this soup like my sons do—without adding anything to it. Obviously they are genetically disposed to know better.

chickpea, tomato and bread soup

Yotam Ottolenghi
Cookbook Author, Chef and Owner, five restaurants and delis, London, UK

Somewhere between a soup and a vegetable stew, this is my take on the Tuscan ribollita. It uses lots of cupboard staples, as well as leftover bread, so you shouldn't need to venture too far to gather together the ingredients. It's a hearty soup: perfect fuel for all the family. Kids love to get involved with making it as well, crushing the chickpeas and tearing apart the bread. Increase or reduce the amount of liquid you add, depending on whether you want it to be more like a soup or a stew.

Makes about 4 servings

6 oz stale sourdough bread (about 3 thick slices), crusts removed
5 Tbsp olive oil, divided
Salt to taste
1 large onion, sliced
1 medium fennel bulb, cored and sliced
3 stalks celery, sliced
1 large carrot, peeled, cut in half lengthwise and sliced
1 Tbsp tomato paste
1 cup white wine
4 cups vegetable stock
1 can (14 oz) whole tomatoes (preferably San Marzano)
2 Tbsp finely chopped parsley
1 Tbsp finely chopped fresh oregano leaves
1 Tbsp fresh thyme leaves
2 tsp granulated sugar
2 bay leaves
Pepper to taste
2 cups chickpeas, cooked or drained from a can
4 Tbsp basil pesto
Extra virgin olive oil for drizzling
Handful of shredded basil leaves for garnish (optional)

1. Preheat the oven to 350°F. Break the bread into chunks with your hands. In a shallow roasting pan, toss the bread chunks with 2 Tbsp of the oil and salt to taste. Bake until the bread chunks are completely dry and crisp, about 10 minutes. Remove from the oven and set aside for later.

2. Meanwhile, heat the remaining oil in a large pot over medium heat. Add the onion and fennel and cook, stirring often, until the onion starts to soften, about 4 minutes.

3. Add the celery and carrot and cook, stirring occasionally, until the carrot starts to soften around the edges, about 4 minutes.

4. Add the tomato paste and cook, stirring, for 1 minute. Add the wine and let it bubble away for a minute or two.

5. Add the stock, tomatoes (with their juices), parsley, oregano, thyme, sugar, bay leaves and salt and pepper to taste. Bring to a boil over medium-high heat. Reduce the heat to medium-low and simmer, covered, until the vegetables are tender, about 30 minutes.

6. About 10 minutes before you want to serve the soup, place the chickpeas in a bowl and crush them a little with a potato masher or the end of a rolling pin; you want some chickpeas to be left whole.

7. Fish out and discard the bay leaves. Add the chickpeas to the soup and simmer for 5 more minutes. Add the reserved bread chunks and stir well. Simmer for 5 more minutes. Taste the soup and season generously with salt and pepper.

8. Ladle the soup into warm bowls. Spoon some pesto in the center of each bowlful, along with a drizzle of olive oil and a scattering of shredded basil (if using).

spicy sweet potato kale soup

Sophie Henderson
Age 17, Victoria, BC

I like this soup because it has a nice spicy aftertaste that makes me want more, and I know it is healthy and very good for me.

Makes about 12 servings

Apple-Sage Stock (recipe follows)
2 to 3 bunches of kale, stems removed and leaves shredded
3 sweet potatoes, peeled and chopped
2 cans (each 15 oz) chickpeas, drained and rinsed
½ onion, chopped
6 cloves garlic, finely chopped

3 Tbsp nutritional yeast (see sidebar)
2 Tbsp minced fresh ginger
½ tsp chili powder
½ tsp ground cumin
¼ tsp dried parsley
¼ tsp salt
¼ tsp liquid smoke
Pepper to taste

1. In a large pot, bring the stock to a boil over high heat. Add all of the remaining ingredients and bring the soup back to a boil. Reduce the heat to medium-low and simmer, uncovered, for at least 1 hour. The longer the soup simmers, the spicier it will be.

2. Ladle the soup into warm bowls and dive in.

Nutritional yeast has a nutty, strong flavor and is often used to give a cheesy flavor to vegan dishes. Look for it in bulk or health food stores.

apple-sage stock

15 cups water
4 carrots, scrubbed and coarsely chopped
3 apples, coarsely chopped
2 onions, coarsely chopped
2 leeks (light green and white parts only), coarsely chopped

2 Tbsp coriander seeds
2 Tbsp whole black peppercorns
5 bay leaves
3 sprigs fresh sage
½ tsp salt

1. In a large pot, combine all of the ingredients. Bring to a boil over high heat. Reduce the heat to medium-low and simmer, partially covered, for 2 to 4 hours.

2. Strain the stock through a fine-mesh sieve, discarding the solids. Let cool, then refrigerate until ready to use.

blt (bacon, lentil and tomato) soup

Scott Riege
Age 14, Calgary, AB

This soup tastes great!

Makes about 6 servings

4 slices bacon, chopped
2 carrots, peeled and chopped
1 onion, finely chopped
2 to 3 cloves garlic, minced
⅓ cup red lentils, rinsed and drained
1½ Tbsp tomato paste
4 cups chicken or vegetable stock, plus a little more if you need to thin the soup
1 can (28 oz) diced or whole tomatoes
½ tsp dried thyme leaves or dried Italian herb seasoning
Salt and pepper to taste
Whipping cream (35% MF; optional)
Croutons or squares of toast for garnish
1 Tbsp shredded lettuce or basil for garnish (optional)

1. In a large pot, cook the bacon over medium-low heat until it starts to get crispy, about 5 minutes. Drain off most of the fat.

2. Add the carrots, onion and garlic to the bacon in the pot. Cook, stirring often, until the onion is softened and the carrots start to soften at the edges, 5 to 10 minutes.

3. Add the lentils and tomato paste. Stir for a few minutes until the paste starts to brown.

4. Add the stock, tomatoes (with their juices), thyme and salt and pepper to taste. Bring to a boil over medium-high heat. Reduce the heat to medium-low and simmer, uncovered, until all the vegetables are tender, about 30 minutes.

5. Remove the pot from the heat. Using an immersion blender in the pot, blend the soup until smooth. Add a little more stock if the soup seems too thick.

6. Ladle the soup into warm bowls. Add a drizzle of cream and a scattering of croutons and lettuce or basil if you wish. Enjoy!

spicy moroccan lentil soup

Jamie Harling
Executive Chef, Deane House Restaurant, Calgary, AB

I was inspired to make this soup following my travels in North Africa. The spice mixture reminds me of the flavors of Morocco, one of my favorite countries in the world. When I came up with this recipe it was also the year of the pulse so it only made sense to produce a lentil soup!

Makes 6 to 8 servings

1 Tbsp cumin seeds
1 Tbsp coriander seeds
¼ tsp whole black peppercorns
5 sprigs fresh thyme
2 whole star anise
2 bay leaves
1 cinnamon stick
3 Tbsp canola oil
1 medium onion, finely chopped
2 stalks celery, finely chopped
2 Roma tomatoes, finely chopped
1 medium carrot, peeled and finely chopped
1 sweet red pepper, roasted (recipe opposite), seeded and finely chopped
1 Tbsp smoked paprika
½ tsp red chili flakes
1½ cups red lentils, rinsed and drained
1 Tbsp tomato paste
½ cup white wine
8 cups water
3 Tbsp cold butter, cubed
3 Tbsp red wine vinegar, or to taste
Salt to taste

1. In a small, dry skillet over medium heat, toast the cumin and coriander seeds and black peppercorns, stirring often, until they begin to release their aromas, about 2 minutes. Remove from the skillet and, once cooled, grind in a spice grinder or clean coffee grinder. Set them aside.

2. Place the thyme sprigs, star anise, bay leaves and cinnamon in a piece of cheesecloth and tie to make a bouquet garni.

3. In a large pot, heat the oil over medium-low heat. Add the onion and cook, stirring often, until it is translucent, about 4 minutes.

4. Add the celery, tomatoes, carrot and roasted pepper. Cook, stirring often, until the vegetables begin to soften, about 5 minutes.

5. Add the ground spices, bouquet garni, paprika and red chili flakes. Then add the lentils and tomato paste and stir quickly, ensuring all the ingredients are combined.

6. Remove the pot from the heat and deglaze with the white wine, stirring to scrape up all the bits from the bottom of the pot. Return the pot to the heat and allow to cook until the liquid has almost evaporated.

7. Add the water and bring to a boil over medium-high heat. Once boiling, reduce the heat to medium-low and simmer, uncovered, until the vegetables and lentils are tender, 20 to 25 minutes.

8. Remove the pot from the heat. Remove the bouquet garni. Using a food processor or immersion blender, purée the soup until smooth. As you are blending, slowly add the butter. Season to taste with red wine vinegar and salt.

9. If the soup is too thick, add a little more water (or vegetable or chicken stock) until the soup achieves a desired consistency. Ladle the soup into warm bowls and enjoy.

Make this soup even heartier by topping each serving with crumbled cooked merguez sausage, crumbled feta or a dollop of salsa verde (a bright sauce made with fresh herbs, capers, anchovies, garlic, oil and lemon).

If you omit the butter, this soup is suitable for vegans.

roasted sweet pepper

1. Preheat the broiler to high. Broil a whole sweet pepper, about 4 inches from the heat and turning often, until completely charred, 10 to 15 minutes. Put the pepper in a bowl and cover with plastic wrap. When the pepper is cool, hold it over a bowl to collect any juices, then peel off the skin and remove the stem, membranes and seeds.

noodling around

THERE'S A REASON CHICKEN SOUP WITH NOODLES IS A CLASSIC
and that's because we all love to noodle around with soup. Slurp them up, spell out secret messages with alphabet noodles or fill up with filled pastas floating in delicious broth. In this chapter, soups stocked up with wiggly noodles and stuffed pastas are the stars. And, because we love rice in soup, we've added some of those, too. Since noodles and rice are loved the whole world over, lots of different cuisines are featured in this chapter, from Italian to Asian to German.

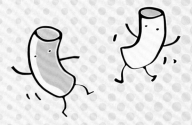

Tomato Beef Macaroni Soup (page 119)

yummy beef and pasta soup

Jaelie Young
Age 9, Calgary, AB

I like this recipe because it is not too spicy and it doesn't take too long to make. Plus, it has noodles—which are my favorite.

Makes about 8 servings

If you use gluten-free macaroni, this soup will be gluten free.

2 Tbsp vegetable oil, divided
1 lb lean ground beef
Salt and pepper to taste
1 cup chopped onion
1 cup peeled and chopped carrot
1 cup chopped celery
3 cloves garlic, minced
3 cups beef stock
1 can (28 oz) diced tomatoes

2 cans (each 8 oz) tomato sauce
1 Tbsp Worcestershire sauce
1 tsp dried basil leaves
1 tsp dried oregano leaves
2 bay leaves
1 cup macaroni pasta
Freshly grated Parmesan cheese for garnish

1. In a large pot, heat 1 Tbsp of the oil over medium-high heat. Add the beef and season with salt and pepper to taste. Cook, stirring often, until the beef has browned, about 5 minutes.

2. Using a slotted spoon, remove the beef from the pot. Pour off and discard the fat in the pot.

3. Heat the remaining oil in the pot and add the onion, carrot, and celery. Cook, stirring often, until the onion has softened, about 8 minutes. Add the garlic and cook, stirring, until it smells good, about 1 minute.

4. Return the beef to the pot, along with the stock, tomatoes (with their juices), tomato sauce, Worcestershire sauce, basil, oregano, bay leaves and more salt and pepper to taste. Bring it all to a boil over medium-high heat.

5. Add the macaroni and reduce the heat to medium. Simmer, uncovered, until the vegetables and macaroni are tender, 15 to 20 minutes. Fish out and discard the bay leaves.

6. Ladle the soup into warm bowls and garnish with a scattering of Parmesan cheese.

tomato beef macaroni soup

Liana Robberecht
Executive Chef, WinSport, Calgary, AB

Growing up, my sister and I were obsessed with our mother's tomato macaroni soup. Constantly requesting it, we loved the hearty flavors and rich aroma. Not much has changed for my sister Holly and me, except now that we're the adults, we cook the soup! Friends, family or just for ourselves, this soup is always a hit with kids. It transports me back in time one spoonful at a time!

The soup should be somewhat thick, but if you'd like it to be more "soupy," add 1 to 2 cups stock or water and heat through.

Makes about 4 servings

2½ lb ground beef
1 large onion, finely chopped
1 clove garlic, minced
3 cups beef stock, plus more as needed
1 can (14 oz) diced tomatoes
3 Tbsp tomato paste
2 tsp dried parsley leaves

½ tsp dried ground oregano
½ tsp each salt and pepper
¼ tsp dried ground rosemary
2 bay leaves
2 cups cooked macaroni pasta
Cold-pressed canola oil (optional; I like
    Highwood Crossing's)

1. In a large pot over medium-high heat, cook the beef, onion and garlic, stirring often, until the beef is no longer pink, about 8 minutes. Remove the pot from the heat and drain off as much fat as you can. (Discard the fat once it cools.)

2. Return the pot to the heat and stir in the stock, tomatoes (with their juices), tomato paste, parsley, oregano, salt, pepper, rosemary and bay leaves. Bring to a boil over medium-high heat. Reduce the heat to medium-low and simmer, covered, for 15 to 20 minutes.

3. Add the cooked pasta and simmer just until the pasta is heated through, about 3 minutes. Fish out and discard the bay leaves. Taste and season with more salt and pepper if necessary.

4. Ladle the soup into warm bowls and, for a grown-up garnish, drizzle with a little cold-pressed canola oil (if using).

dragon soup

Mrs. Foster's Grade 2 Class 2015–2016
West Kelowna, BC

The secret to making dragon soup is a dragon needs to be the chef. In our class, the smallest child wears a dragon costume when we make this soup.

Makes about 6 servings

6 beef bouillon cubes
6 cups water
1 lb stew beef, cubed
2 Tbsp all-purpose flour
Salt and pepper to taste
2 Tbsp vegetable oil
1 tsp dried herbs of your choice (see method) or 2 bay leaves
1 large onion, finely chopped
3 carrots, peeled and finely chopped
3 potatoes, peeled and finely chopped

2 stalks celery, finely chopped
½ cup yellow or green beans, chopped
¼ cup pearl or pot barley, rinsed and drained
½ cup alphabet noodles or macaroni pasta
½ cup frozen or drained, canned corn kernels
½ cup frozen peas
Dinner buns to serve

If the soup is too runny for your liking, scoop a ladleful of the soup into a small bowl. Whisk in a little all-purpose flour until the mixture is smooth. Add the flour mixture back to the soup and simmer, stirring often, until the soup thickens, about 3 minutes.

1. In a large pot, dissolve the bouillon cubes in the water, then bring to a boil over high heat.

2. Meanwhile, toss the beef in the flour and salt and pepper to taste until the beef is well coated. In a large skillet, heat the oil over medium-high heat. Add the beef and cook, turning occasionally, until the beef cubes are browned on all sides, about 8 minutes.

3. Transfer the beef to the large pot, along with any other seasonings you like, such as dried oregano, tarragon or basil leaves or a couple of bay leaves.

4. Bring the stock back to a boil over medium-high heat. Reduce the heat to medium-low and simmer, uncovered, until the beef is tender, about 1 hour.

5. Add the onion, carrots, potatoes, celery, beans and barley. Bring the soup back to a boil. Reduce the heat to medium-low and simmer, uncovered, until the barley and vegetables are almost tender, about 10 minutes.

6. Add the noodles, corn and peas and simmer until the barley, noodles and vegetables are tender, about 15 minutes. Fish out and discard the bay leaves (if using), then season with salt and pepper to taste.

7. Ladle the hearty soup into warm bowls and serve with dinner buns.

slurpy udon noodle soup with bok choy

Julie Cove
Cookbook Author and Nutritionist

What I love about this soup is that there's a good balance of greens to noodles, the soup provides vegetable protein (the edamame or tofu) and it is easy as pie! It's a great make-ahead recipe, too. If you prep the veggies and/or tofu and cook the noodles but don't add them to the broth, you can refrigerate all three separately. When you're ready to serve, just reheat the broth, add the veggies, and drop in the noodles at the last minute to heat them through. I do this in the morning and pop the soup in a thermos so it's nice and warm for my kid's lunch.

Makes 4 servings

4 cups water (preferably filtered, alkaline water)
3 Tbsp liquid protein concentrate (see sidebar), or to taste
1 clove garlic, minced
1 tsp minced fresh ginger
⅛ tsp salt
1½ cups shelled edamame beans or 4 oz

firm tofu, cut into ½-inch cubes (both preferably organic)
8 oz spelt udon noodles or 2 to 3 bundles of buckwheat soba noodles
2 to 3 cups chopped baby bok choy (leaves and stalks)
Finely chopped chives or green onions for garnish (optional)

1. In a medium pot, combine the water, liquid protein concentrate, garlic, ginger and salt and stir well. Bring to a simmer over medium heat.

2. Add the edamame or tofu and simmer, uncovered, until heated through, the edamame for 4 to 5 minutes, the tofu for about 3 minutes.

3. Meanwhile, bring a large pot of water to a boil over high heat. Add the noodles and cook according to the package directions until they are al dente. Drain the noodles and rinse well under warm, running water.

4. Add the bok choy to the pot containing the edamame (or tofu). Simmer just until it wilts, about 1 minute. Remove the pot from the heat.

5. Divide the noodles evenly among four soup bowls. Using a slotted spoon, scoop the edamame (or tofu) and bok choy from the pot and divide them among the bowls of noodles. Pour the soup evenly over each serving. Garnish with a bright scattering of chives (if using).

This recipe is adapted from Eat Better, Live Better, Feel Better *(Appetite by Random House, 2016).*

Liquid protein concentrate is a source of plant protein usually made from soybeans; my favorite brand is Bragg Liquid Aminos. It's used to add flavor to all kinds of different dishes and as an alternative to soy sauce or tamari. Look for it in health food stores.

Serve this soup with a side salad of lightly dressed mixed greens or some raw veggie sticks to increase the alkalinity of your meal.

spaghetti and mini meatball soup

Bonnie Stern
Cookbook Author and Food Columnist

This fun, delicious soup brings out the kid in all of us. It's a perfect main course and kids love the tiny meatballs.

Makes about 4 main-course or 6 appetizer-size servings

meatballs
1 lb ground beef
½ cup panko bread crumbs
1 large egg
2 Tbsp finely chopped parsley
2 Tbsp ketchup
1 Tbsp Worcestershire sauce
1½ tsp salt

soup
2 Tbsp olive oil
1 large carrot, peeled and finely chopped
1 stalk celery, finely chopped
1 small onion, finely chopped
4 cups chicken stock (preferably unsalted)
1 can (14 oz) diced tomatoes
2 tsp salt, divided
3 oz thin egg noodles (about 2 inches long) or broken-up angel-hair noodles
Pepper to taste
½ cup shaved Parmesan cheese
2 Tbsp finely chopped parsley

When making this soup ahead, don't add the noodles until you reheat the meatballs and stock.

If you have leftover soup, the noodles will absorb more liquid, so add a little water when reheating and season again with salt and pepper to taste.

1. For the meatballs, mix together the ground beef, bread crumbs, egg, parsley, ketchup, Worcestershire sauce and salt in a medium bowl. Knead gently until thoroughly combined.

2. Shape the beef mixture into approximately 80 tiny meatballs, using about 1 tsp for each ball. As each is shaped, place in a single layer on a large rimmed baking sheet lined with parchment paper or aluminum foil. (Make sure the meatballs are a safe size for the children who will be eating them; for very young children, you may have to cut them into smaller pieces before serving.) Refrigerate the meatballs until ready to cook.

3. For the soup, heat the oil in a large pot over medium heat. Add the carrot, celery and onion and cook, stirring often, until the onion starts to soften, about 5 minutes.

Ground chicken can be used instead of ground beef. If the raw meatball mixture is very soft, add more bread crumbs and refrigerate the chicken mixture to firm it up before shaping the meatballs.

For a vegetarian version, add cubes of firm or extra-firm tofu instead of meatballs.

For a gluten-free version, use gluten-free quick-cooking oats or gluten-free bread crumbs instead of regular bread crumbs and thin rice noodles instead of egg noodles.

4. Add the stock and tomatoes (with their juices) and bring to a boil over medium-high heat. Add half of the salt. (If using salted chicken stock, add salt at the end of cooking only if needed.)

5. Gently add the meatballs to the pot. Bring just to a boil. Reduce the heat to medium-low and cook, uncovered and occasionally stirring very gently, for 10 minutes.

6. Add the noodles to the pot. Bring back to a simmer and cook until the noodles are tender, about 10 minutes. Season the soup with salt and pepper to taste.

7. Ladle the soup into warm bowls and serve with a generous sprinkle of cheese and parsley.

souper douper chicken tortellini soup

Julia Mackenzie Martin
Age 11, Calgary, AB

I love to cook. I go to summer cooking camps at the Southern Alberta Institute of Technology (SAIT) in Calgary each year. Recently, a highlight was attending the Pastry Chef Showcase in Calgary. Did I mention I have a sweet tooth?

This colorful, heartwarming soup has strong Italian flavors. Tomatoes and spinach brighten and warm up any table on a cool day. The savory flavor of the cheese tortellini and Parmesan cheese balances the sweetness of the tomatoes perfectly. Lastly, this recipe has all of the four food groups! See if you can identify them.

Try this soup with about 2 cups of cubed leftover roast turkey instead of chicken. You can also substitute frozen spinach for fresh.

Makes about 8 servings

2 Tbsp olive oil, divided
2 boneless, skinless chicken breasts, cut into small pieces
1 onion, finely chopped
3 cloves garlic, minced
9 cups chicken stock

1 can (28 oz) diced or crushed tomatoes (drained)
2 Tbsp dried Italian herb seasoning
9 oz fresh or frozen cheese tortellini
3 cups lightly packed chopped spinach
1 cup freshly grated Parmesan cheese for garnish

1. In a large pot, heat half of the oil over medium-high heat. Add the chicken and cook, stirring, until browned on all sides, about 5 minutes (chicken may still be pink inside). Using a slotted spoon, remove the chicken from the pot and set aside in a bowl.

2. Add the remaining olive oil to the pot and reduce the heat to medium. Add the onion and cook, stirring often, until it is soft and translucent, about 8 minutes. Add the garlic and cook, stirring, until the garlic is browned and caramelized, about 3 minutes.

3. Add the stock, tomatoes and herbs, then bring to a boil over medium-high heat. Reduce the heat to medium-low and simmer, uncovered, for 20 minutes.

4. Increase the heat to medium-high and stir in the tortellini. Follow the cooking instructions on the package but undercook the pasta by about 5 minutes.

5. Reduce the heat to low. Add the browned chicken and simmer until the chicken is no longer pink inside and the pasta is cooked, about 10 minutes.

6. Add the spinach and simmer just until the spinach has wilted, about 2 minutes.

7. Ladle the soup into warm bowls and serve sprinkled with Parmesan cheese.

homemade chicken and rice soup

Curtis Stone
Award-Winning Chef, Author and Television Personality

Whenever I'm feeling under the weather, I turn to this soul-hugging chicken soup, which is especially hearty with the addition of rice. While classic recipes have carrots, celery and onions, I like to add veggies like celery root and turnip for a unique edge. Dunk in a slice of cheesy toast or buttered bread if you're feeling particularly peckish.

Makes about 8 servings

1 lemon
1 whole chicken (about 4 lb), trimmed of
    excess fat
8 cups water
1 sprig thyme
1 bay leaf
1 medium onion, chopped (about
    1½ cups)

2 carrots, peeled and chopped (about
    1½ cups)
1 medium celery root, peeled and
    chopped (about 3 cups)
1 white turnip, peeled and chopped
    (about 2 cups)
¾ cup uncooked long-grain white rice
Salt and pepper to taste
1 Tbsp finely chopped parsley

1. Using a vegetable peeler, pare the yellow zest from the lemon (avoiding the white pith) and put it in a large, heavy pot. Reserve the lemon.

2. Using a large sharp knife, cut the chicken into eight pieces (two drumsticks, two thighs, two wings, and two breasts), reserving the carcass.

3. Place the chicken and carcass in the pot. Add the water, thyme and bay leaf and bring to a simmer over medium-high heat, skimming off the foam that rises to the surface. Reduce the heat to medium-low and simmer gently, uncovered, until the chicken is just cooked through, about 45 minutes.

4. Using tongs, transfer the chicken pieces to a large bowl and set aside until they are cool enough to handle. Set the stock aside.

5. Remove the chicken meat from the bones and discard the skin, bones and cartilage. Coarsely shred the meat into bite-size pieces.

6. Remove the chicken carcass, herbs and lemon zest from the stock and discard them.

7. Add the onion, carrots, celery root and turnip to the pot of stock and bring to a simmer over medium-high heat. Reduce the heat to medium-low and simmer, uncovered, until the vegetables begin to soften, about 10 minutes.

8. Stir in the rice and continue cooking until the vegetables and rice are tender, about 12 minutes. Add the cooked chicken and simmer for 5 minutes.

9. Squeeze in the juice from the reserved lemon. Season with salt and pepper to taste.

10. Ladle the soup into warm bowls, sprinkle with parsley, and revel in the comfort.

spicy lemony pork-noodle soup

Jesse Gunn
Age 13, jessegunnrocks.com, New York City, NY

This soup is comforting and delicious.

Makes 2 servings

Korean barbecue sauce is a sticky, pungent barbecue sauce. Look for it in Asian grocery stores.

Agave nectar is a liquid sweetener derived from the agave plant. Look for it in health food stores.

½ lb ground pork
1 Tbsp sesame oil, plus more to taste
½ stalk lemongrass, cut into 3 equal pieces
1 clove garlic, minced
1 tsp Korean barbecue sauce (see sidebar)
1 tsp agave nectar (see sidebar)
Salt and pepper to taste
8 oz or 2 bundles Asian long-life noodles (see sidebar)
Lemony Chicken Stock (recipe opposite)
1 stalk Chinese broccoli or bok choy, cut into 2-inch pieces
2 to 4 shiitake mushrooms (optional)
2 hard- or soft-boiled eggs, cut in half (optional)
Finely chopped green onions for garnish
2 lime wedges for serving

1. Pat the ground pork dry with paper towels. In a small skillet, heat 1 Tbsp sesame oil over medium-high heat. Add the pork and lemongrass and cook, stirring to break up the lumps of pork, until the pork is no longer pink, about 3 minutes.

2. Once the pork starts to get brown and a little crispy, add the garlic and barbecue sauce and cook, stirring, until it smells good, about 1 minute.

3. Scrape the pork into a bowl. Fish out and discard the lemongrass. Add the agave nectar and a dash of sesame oil to the pork. Taste the pork and adjust the seasonings, adding salt and pepper to taste or a little more agave to sweeten it, if necessary.

4. Bring a large saucepan of water to a boil over high heat. Add the noodles and cook for 3 to 4 minutes; they should be firm and not mushy. Drain well and set aside.

5. Add the stock to the now-empty saucepan and bring to a boil over high heat. Add the broccoli and shiitake mushrooms (if using) and cook until the broccoli changes to a dark green, about 2 to 3 minutes.

6. Divide the cooked noodles between two warm bowls. Ladle in the stock, making sure to divide the greens and mushrooms (if using), evenly. Top each serving with the pork. Add an egg to each bowl if you like, then scatter with green onions. Serve with a lime wedge on the side for squeezing over the soup.

lemony chicken stock

1 to 2 stalks lemongrass
4 cups chicken stock (approx.)
1 cup water
½ lime, cut in half
1 green onion, coarsely chopped
2 Tbsp soy sauce
½ tsp minced garlic
A splash of rice vinegar
Pepper to taste
Chicken bouillon powder (optional)

Known as *yi mein*, Asian long-life noodles are usually found in the chiller with the other refrigerated noodles in your local Asian grocery stores. Don't be tempted to cook the noodles in the lemony chicken stock. Doing this will make the soup cloudy and the alkaline from the noodles will change its flavor.

1. Lightly pound one stalk of lemongrass to release the flavors, then cut the stalk into 3-inch pieces. Put the pieces of lemongrass in a large pot.

2. Add the 4 cups chicken stock, the water, lime, green onion, soy sauce, garlic, vinegar and pepper to taste. Bring to a boil over medium-high heat, then boil the stock for 5 minutes.

3. Taste the stock and adjust the seasonings, if necessary. If it doesn't taste chickeny enough, dissolve a little chicken bouillon powder in the stock; if it doesn't taste lemony enough, add the remaining stalk of lemongrass and boil the stock for 2 more minutes; if the stock tastes too lemony, add a little more stock.

4. Drain the stock, discarding the solids. Let the stock cool, then refrigerate until ready to use.

mitchell's ham and orzo soup

Mitchell Loxton
Age 12, Orillia, ON

This tastes great because the ham in the soup is yummy and the spices go well together.

Makes about 4 servings

1 Tbsp canola oil
3 carrots, peeled and finely chopped
2 stalks celery, finely chopped
1 onion, finely chopped
1 clove garlic, minced
6 cups beef stock
1½ cups chopped ham
½ cup frozen peas
¼ cup orzo pasta
1 tsp crushed dried rosemary leaves
½ tsp ground cumin
Salt and pepper to taste

1. In a large pot, heat the oil over medium heat. Add the carrots, celery and onion and cook, stirring often, until the onion starts to soften, about 5 minutes. Add the garlic and cook, stirring, until it smells good, about 1 minute.

2. Add the stock, ham, peas, orzo, rosemary, cumin and salt and pepper to taste. Bring to a boil over medium-high heat. Reduce the heat to medium-low and simmer, uncovered, until the vegetables and orzo are tender, about 7 minutes.

3. Ladle the soup into warm bowls and serve!

classic chicken noodle soup

Jamie Kennedy
Chef and Owner, Jamie Kennedy Kitchens, Hillier, ON

Chicken soup carries a strong message of healing and restorative power. Grandmothers and chefs alike know that it is medicine for the soul and body and have been treating their families and guests with this elixir for centuries.

Makes about 6 servings

1 whole chicken (about 5 lb), trimmed of excess fat	3 sprigs thyme
12 cups chicken stock (approx.)	1 tsp whole black peppercorns
2 carrots, peeled and finely chopped	3 whole cloves
2 stalks celery, finely chopped	4 oz linguine noodles
1 leek (light green and white part only), finely chopped	Salt and pepper to taste
	2 green onions, thinly sliced diagonally (optional)

1. Place the chicken in a large, deep pot and add the chicken stock. The chicken should be covered by the stock so add more stock if necessary. Slowly bring to a boil over medium-high heat. Reduce the heat to medium-low and simmer, partially covered, for 2 hours.

2. Remove the chicken from the pot, reserving the stock in the pot. Set the chicken aside to cool.

3. When the chicken is cool enough to handle, break it up, discarding the skin. Shred the breast and leg meat and set aside for later.

4. Put the carcass and chicken bones back into the pot. Bring the stock back to a simmer over medium-high heat. Reduce the heat to medium-low and simmer, uncovered, for 2 hours. Strain the stock through a fine-mesh sieve, discarding the bones and carcass.

5. Pour the stock back into the pot and bring to a boil over medium-high heat. Add the reserved shredded chicken meat, the carrots, celery, leek, thyme, peppercorns and cloves to the pot. Reduce the heat to medium-low and simmer, uncovered, until the vegetables are tender, about 20 minutes.

6. Add the noodles and simmer, uncovered, until they are tender, about 8 minutes. Season with salt and pepper to taste.

7. Ladle the soup into warm bowls and garnish with a drift of chopped green onions (if using).

mushroom soup with "grubs" (spaetzle)

Lindsay Anderson and Dana VanVeller
Cookbook Authors and Creators of FEAST: An Edible Road Trip (edibleroadtrip.com)

This soup is a great way to introduce kids to the wonderful world of mushrooms, both cultivated and wild. It's also full of easy-to-make spaetzle, the oh-so satisfying German egg noodles that look like worms! It's a fun project that creates a hearty meal—perfect for a rainy day.

You can also add dried mushrooms (like morels, chanterelles or porcini) to this soup. Simply rehydrate them by pouring just enough boiling water over them to cover, and let soak for about 5 minutes. Don't throw away the soaking water when you're done—it's full of flavor, and up to ¼ cup of it can go into the pot along with the stock.

Makes about 4 servings

soup
1½ Tbsp butter
1 Tbsp olive oil
2 large shallots, finely chopped
2 cloves garlic, minced
2 large carrots, finely chopped
2 large stalks celery, finely chopped
1½ lb mixed mushrooms, sliced (see sidebar)
6 cups chicken or vegetable stock
1½ cups whole milk (3.25% MF)
2 tsp salt
½ tsp pepper
½ cup finely chopped parsley

spaetzle
2 large eggs
3 Tbsp whole milk (3.25% MF)
1 tsp salt
1 cup all-purpose flour

1. For the soup, heat the butter and olive oil in a large pot over medium heat. Add the shallots and cook, stirring, for about 2 minutes. Add the garlic and cook, stirring, until it smells good, 3 to 4 minutes.

2. Stir in the carrots and celery and cook, stirring occasionally, until the vegetables start to soften, 7 to 8 minutes.

3. Stir in the mushrooms. Cook, stirring occasionally, until the vegetables and mushrooms have softened, 8 to 10 minutes.

4. Add the stock, milk, salt and pepper and increase the heat to medium-high. Taste the soup and season with more salt and pepper if necessary. Cover and let the soup come to a boil.

5. While the soup is heating up, make the spaetzle dough. In a medium bowl, whisk together the eggs, milk and salt. Gradually stir in the flour until well combined. Set aside until the soup is boiling and/or you're ready to serve.

6. Spoon half of the dough into a spaetzle maker or a sturdy colander set over the pot of boiling soup. Follow the manufacturer's instructions for using the spaetzle maker or, if using a colander, use a wooden spoon or rubber spatula to press the dough through the holes of the colander. Shake the colander so the noodles fall directly into the pot, or use a butter knife to scrape them off. Repeat with the remaining dough. The spaetzle are fully cooked about 1 minute after they hit the boiling soup, so once you've used up the dough, stir in the parsley and remove the pot from the heat.

7. Ladle the soup into warm bowls and enjoy fishing for the "grubs."

real greek egg-lemon soup

Christine Cushing
Chef and TV Personality

If there is one soup that reminds me of being a kid, it's this classic Greek egg-lemon soup. My dad used to make it for us when we were kids and now it's one of my favorites. Only the best-quality chicken stock will do here. If you like, substitute rice for the orzo pasta and make it gluten-free.

Makes about 4 servings

8 cups chicken stock
¾ cup orzo pasta or rice
2 large eggs
Juice of 1 lemon
Salt and pepper to taste

1. In a medium pot, bring the stock to a boil. Add the orzo and simmer, uncovered, until the pasta is cooked, about 10 minutes.

2. In a medium bowl, whisk together the eggs and lemon juice until frothy.

3. Scoop out a ladleful of the hot stock from the pot, put it into a measuring cup, then, whisking the egg mixture vigorously, gradually drizzle in the hot stock. Pour this mixture back into the hot soup.

4. Immediately remove the pot from the heat (do not let the soup boil). Season with salt and pepper to taste.

5. Ladle the soup into warm bowls and serve immediately.

sweet pea and tortellini soup with parmesan

Caren McSherry
Cookbook Author and Owner, The Gourmet Warehouse, Vancouver, BC

Cheese tortellini in a delicious broth makes for a satisfying lunch or dinner. Kids love grated Parmesan cheese—and plenty of it—to sprinkle on the top.

Makes about 6 servings

1 Tbsp olive oil
1 shallot, finely chopped
1 clove garlic, minced
8 cups chicken or vegetable stock
3 cups frozen cheese tortellini or ravioli (I like mini tortellini)
1 cup frozen peas
1 tsp finely grated lemon zest
2 Tbsp finely chopped parsley
Salt to taste
Freshly grated Parmesan cheese to serve

1. In a large pot, heat the oil over medium heat. Add the shallot and garlic and cook, covered, until the shallot has softened, about 4 minutes.

2. Add the stock and bring to a boil over medium-high heat. Add the tortellini or ravioli and cook until tender, about 12 minutes.

3. Add the peas, lemon zest and parsley and turn the heat off. The peas will cook in 3 minutes. Season with salt to taste.

4. Ladle the soup into warm bowls and pass the Parmesan.

italian wedding soup

Emily Grace
Age 17, Blogger, Kissimmee, FL

This is the perfect soup for all occasions. Use gluten-free bread crumbs and gluten-free pasta and it fits with a gluten-free diet.

I have my own website, EmilysKitchenasium.com, and I host my own YouTube channel called Emily's Kitchenasium. I recently did my 100th episode and it was a bloopers special!

This is my great-grandma's soup recipe and I make it now with my nana, her daughter. This soup is very special because it is a family tradition and having family traditions is a way to keep close to the ones you love. It brings back special memories every time we eat it. I love that my nana passed on her mother's family soup recipe to me.

Makes about 8 servings

meatballs
½ lb ground turkey
½ lb ground beef
½ cup fresh bread crumbs
¼ cup Pecorino Romano cheese, plus more for garnish
1 large egg
1 Tbsp finely chopped parsley
2 cloves garlic, minced
Salt and pepper to taste

soup
2 Tbsp olive oil
4 carrots, peeled and finely chopped
3 stalks celery, finely chopped
1 large onion, finely chopped
3 cloves garlic, minced
10 cups chicken stock
2 cups lightly packed chopped spinach
1 cup small pasta of your choice or pearl or pot barley, rinsed and drained

1. For the meatballs, mix together the ground turkey and beef, bread crumbs, cheese, egg, parsley, garlic, and salt and pepper to taste in a medium bowl until well combined.

2. Form the mixture into small meatballs about the size of a nickel. Arrange the meatballs in a single layer on a large rimmed baking sheet and refrigerate until ready to use.

3. For the soup, heat the olive oil in a large pot over medium heat. Add the carrots, celery and onion and cook, stirring often, until the onions are translucent, about 4 minutes. Add the garlic and cook, stirring, until it smells good, about 1 minute.

4. Add the stock and spinach and bring to a simmer over medium heat. Simmer, uncovered, until the vegetables are tender, about 30 minutes.

5. Bring the soup to a boil over medium-high heat and gradually add the meatballs. Add the pasta, then reduce the heat to medium-low and simmer, covered, until the meatballs are no longer pink inside and the pasta is tender, about 30 minutes.

6. Ladle the soup into warm bowls and sprinkle with more cheese on top.

mixed bean soup with farfalline

Tanya Bastianich Manuali
Cookbook Author, Chef and TV Personality

We use cannellini
and kidney beans
as the base for this
soup because they
take about the same
time to cook, but you
could substitute other
beans as long as their
cooking times are
similar (chickpeas take
longer than all other
beans, so don't use
those).

If you are making this
soup ahead of time,
prepare it up to the
point where you add
the farfalline. Reheat
gently and cook the
pasta in the soup right
before serving.

If using gluten-free
pasta here, cook it
separately, until very
al dente, and stir it in
gently before serving.

I cannot remember a weekend morning when I was living in my mom's house when I did not wake up to something percolating on the stove. A tomato sauce for lunch or a chicken soup to warm the heart were common, but even more often, my mother spent the morning preparing a vegetable minestra, loaded with lots of healthy beans. My mom's soups are the best; she cooks each big pot with care, adding in loads of different vegetables—typically from her garden—at different and correct times so that she ends up with a smooth, velvety and soul-soothing pot of soup that our entire family loves.

Makes 6 servings

4 Tbsp olive oil, divided
2 medium carrots, peeled and chopped
2 celery stalks, chopped
1 medium onion, chopped
1 Tbsp fresh thyme leaves, chopped
4 cloves garlic, finely chopped
3 Tbsp tomato paste
3 quarts water (approx.)
3-inch piece Grana Padano cheese rind
2 bay leaves (preferably fresh)

½ cup dried cannellini beans, soaked and drained (see page 8)
½ cup dried kidney beans, soaked and drained (see page 8)
1 small head escarole, chopped
½ cup brown lentils, rinsed and drained
Salt and pepper to taste
1 cup farfalline pasta (tiny bow ties; see sidebar)
1 cup parsley leaves, finely chopped
6 Tbsp freshly grated Grana Padano cheese

1. In a large pot or Dutch oven, heat 3 Tbsp of the oil over medium heat. Add the carrots, celery and onion and cook, stirring often, until the onion is softened, about 8 minutes. Add the thyme and garlic and cook, stirring, until they smell good, about 1 minute.

2. Push the vegetables to the edges of the pot and spoon the tomato paste into the space in the middle. Let the paste cook, without stirring, for a minute or two, then stir it into the vegetables.

3. Add 3 quarts water, the cheese rind and bay leaves. Bring to a simmer and add the beans. Cook, covered, until the beans are almost tender, 50 minutes to 1 hour.

4. Add the escarole and lentils and simmer, uncovered, until the beans and lentils are tender, 25 to 35 minutes. Season with salt and pepper to taste. If the soup seems very thick, add 1 to 2 cups more water.

5. Add the farfalline and parsley and cook until very al dente, then remove the pot from the heat (the pasta will cook more in the pot off the heat as you get ready to serve it). Fish out and discard the bay leaves. Stir in the remaining 1 Tbsp olive oil.

6. Ladle the soup into warm bowls, sprinkling each serving with 1 Tbsp grated Grana Padano.

This recipe is adapted from Healthy Pasta *by Joseph Bastianich and Tanya Bastianich Manuali (Appetite by Random House, 2015).*

the main event

BEEF AND BARLEY AND FISH CHOWDER ARE CLASSIC SOUPS FOR A
reason. Who doesn't love a hearty, rib-sticking soup? But how about a soup that tastes like
pizza? Or one inspired by a cheeseburger? This chapter has all sorts of soups packed with
chicken, beef, pork, fish or seafood. From chowders that feature the bounty of the sea to soups
that are hearty enough to be mistaken for a stew, you'll be happy to let these soups take a
starring role.

White Bean, Cabbage and Sausage Soup (page 157)

pizza soup

Michael Smith
Cookbook Author and Chef

Sometimes it takes good public relations and marketing to sell a healthy dinner to your kids. That's what this soup is all about. The name alone will tempt any tentative taster, and once they dive into the familiar fun flavors, they'll never notice it's really a bowl of homemade goodness.

The flavors of pizza are great no matter how you mix them up, so feel free to add whatever pizza ingredients you like: sliced sweet peppers, mushrooms, pitted olives and/or cooked bacon are all good.

Makes about 4 servings

2 Tbsp olive oil
2 onions, chopped
6 to 8 cloves garlic, minced
4 cups chicken stock or water
1 can (28 oz) crushed tomatoes
3 cups or so of your favorite pizza toppings (see sidebar)

4 oz spicy pepperoni, thinly sliced into half-moons
1 Tbsp dried oregano leaves
Salt and pepper to taste
4 to 6 slices of your favorite multigrain bread
8 to 12 oz shredded mozzarella or pizza-blend cheese

1. In a large pot, heat the oil over medium-high heat. Add the onions and garlic and cook, stirring often, until the onions start to soften, 2 or 3 minutes.

2. Add the stock, tomatoes, your chosen pizza toppings, pepperoni, oregano and salt and pepper to taste (you may not need any salt). Bring to a boil over medium-high heat. Let boil vigorously for a moment, then immediately reduce the heat to medium-low to maintain a slow, steady simmer. Cook, covered and stirring occasionally, until the flavors brighten and the textures soften, 10 minutes or so.

3. While the soup simmers, preheat the broiler to high and toast the bread on both sides. (Don't switch off the broiler.) Trim the slices to fit into ovenproof bowls. Set the slices of toast aside and put the bowls on a large rimmed baking sheet.

4. Ladle the soup into the bowls. Top each serving with a slice of toast. Add a thick topping of cheese, then broil until the cheese deliciously melts and browns, 5 minutes or so. Keep an eye on it, moving or turning the baking sheet as needed for even browning. Serve and share!

This recipe is adapted from Family Meals: 100 Easy Everyday Recipes *(Penguin Canada, 2014).*

granny's garlic sausage soup

Alison Lapczuk
Soup Sister

Chicken noodle soup, step aside! My granny's soup will cure all ills, filling both belly and soul. My sometimes-picky 5- and 7-year-old boys, Sam and Eliott, devour this soup. Eliott's face lights up when I make the "really good soup." I like to let my kids snack on extra pieces of carrots or celery while I cook. Kids can help with this recipe by measuring out and rinsing the barley and water. I am proud to share my grandmother Anna Maria Johanson's recipe. Enjoy!

Makes about 4 servings

½ cup pearl or pot barley, rinsed and drained
1 tsp olive oil
1¼ lb hot Italian sausages, cut into bite-size pieces
1 large onion, finely chopped
5 cloves garlic (or more), minced
8 cups beef stock
5 medium Yukon Gold potatoes, peeled and finely chopped
2 large carrots, peeled and finely chopped
Salt and pepper to taste

1. Cook the barley according to the instructions on the package. Drain and set aside to use later.

2. In a large pot, heat the oil over medium heat. Add the sausage and cook, stirring occasionally, until the pieces are browned on all sides (the sausage might still be pink in the middle).

3. Add the onion and cook, stirring often, until lightly browned, about 10 minutes. Add the garlic and cook, stirring, until it smells good, about 1 minute.

4. Add the stock, potatoes and carrots and bring to a boil over medium-high heat. Reduce the heat to medium-low and simmer, covered, until the sausages are cooked and the vegetables are tender, about 30 minutes.

5. Add the cooked barley to the soup and season with salt and pepper to taste.

6. Ladle the soup into warm bowls and enjoy a hearty lunch or supper.

The basic flavors of this soup come from the sausages and broth (and the garlic, of course). You can make many substitutions or additions to this soup. In fact, Granny never used a recipe and neither do I! This is a great opportunity to get kids to pick what goes in. You can use celery rather than carrots, or a can of red kidney beans (drained and rinsed) rather than potatoes. We sometimes add a 28-ounce can of crushed tomatoes for flavor and additional liquid. We also discovered that this soup is amazing when made with duck stock. The sky is the limit— just don't leave out the garlic!

souper douper hamburger soup

Sheldon Kennedy, O.C., A.O.E.

Former NHL player, Co-Founder, Respect Group, and Lead Director of Sheldon Kennedy Child Advocacy Centre, Calgary, AB

This soup (invented by my partner Shannon) has all my favorites in it and it's healthy and hearty. After a long day helping kids who have been hurt, I need it to recharge. This soup helps me to stay strong.

Makes about 6 servings

1 Tbsp coconut oil
1 large red onion, finely chopped
2 lb extra-lean ground beef
1 jar (24 oz) passata, divided (see sidebar)
2 Tbsp dried Italian herb seasoning
Salt and pepper to taste
2 cans (each 28 oz) diced tomatoes
2 lb baby potatoes, scrubbed and halved or quartered
4 large carrots, peeled and chopped
6 stalks celery, chopped
½ cup pearl or pot barley, rinsed and drained
4 cups beef stock
Buttered sourdough bread to serve (optional)

Passata is uncooked tomato purée that has had the skins and seeds strained from it. It has a pure tomato flavor and is the key ingredient in this soup, so don't skip it! Look for passata in the pasta sauce aisle of larger supermarkets or in specialty or Italian grocery stores.

1. In a large skillet, heat the oil over medium-low heat. Add the onion and cook, stirring often, until it is nicely browned, about 12 minutes.

2. Add the ground beef and cook, stirring and breaking up any larger lumps of beef, until the beef is no longer pink, about 8 minutes.

3. Stir in half of the passata, the Italian herb seasoning and salt and pepper to taste.

4. In a slow cooker, combine the tomatoes (with their juices), potatoes, carrots, celery and barley. Top with the ground beef mixture.

5. Add the stock and the rest of the passata to the slow cooker and stir like crazy. Turn the slow cooker to low heat and cook for 7 hours. Stir again.

6. Ladle the soup into warm bowls and serve with buttered sourdough bread for dunking. Yum!

kitchen sink chicken soup

Jann Arden
Singer, Songwriter, Broadcaster and Author

This is very easy, very healthy and very yummy!

Makes about 6 servings

4 Tbsp coconut or olive oil
2 boneless, skinless chicken breasts, cut into bite-size pieces
1 can (19 oz) black beans, drained and rinsed
2 carrots, peeled and finely chopped
2 stalks celery, finely chopped
1 sweet red pepper, seeded and finely chopped
1 small onion, finely chopped
Handful of finely chopped parsley or chives
4 cloves garlic, minced
½ tsp ground cinnamon
¼ tsp cayenne
6 cups chicken stock
Salt and pepper to taste

1. In a large pot, heat the oil over medium heat. Add the chicken, beans, carrots, celery, red pepper, onion, parsley, garlic, cinnamon and cayenne. Cook, stirring constantly, for 10 minutes.

2. Add the chicken stock and season with salt and pepper to taste. Bring to a boil over medium-high heat. Reduce the heat to low and cook, partially covered, for 90 minutes.

3. Ladle the soup into bowls and eat!

"kai palo" five-spice soup with eggs and pork belly

Pailin Chongchitnant
Cookbook Author and YouTuber, hot-thai-kitchen.com

Dark soy sauce is aged longer than regular soy sauce and usually contains molasses or some other sweetener.

Tofu puffs are a type of fried tofu that's light and airy on the inside. It is especially adept at absorbing flavorful broth. Look for tofu puffs in Asian grocery stores, or substitute any other type of fried tofu.

When I was in elementary school in Thailand, Kai Palo was one of my favorite things to eat at the school cafeteria, which always served a wide variety of freshly cooked traditional Thai dishes. Hard-boiled eggs, tofu, and tender braised pork are simmered in a richly flavored salty-sweet broth infused with aromatic spices. This soup is always poured over jasmine rice, because the flavors are too strong to be eaten alone. I have modified this recipe slightly from the original version in my cookbook to make it a bit easier so that you can get the kids involved.

Makes about 4 servings

1½ lb pork belly or pork butt, cut into 1½-inch cubes
1 tsp salt
2 Tbsp vegetable oil
5 cups unsalted pork or chicken stock (approx.)
¼ cup packed palm sugar or brown sugar
3 Tbsp soy sauce
1½ Tbsp dark soy sauce (see sidebar)
1 Tbsp oyster sauce
4 cloves garlic, crushed
¼ tsp pepper
10 cilantro stems (save the leaves for garnish)
8 whole cloves
2 whole star anise
2 cinnamon sticks
1 tsp coriander seeds, toasted
½ tsp whole Sichuan peppercorns, toasted (optional)
Water if needed
4 to 8 large eggs (1 to 2 per person)
12 tofu puffs (see sidebar)
Cooked jasmine rice for serving
Finely chopped cilantro for garnish

1. Toss the pork in the salt to coat well.

2. In a large, heavy-bottomed pot, heat the oil over medium-high heat. Cooking in batches so as not to crowd the pot, cook the pork until browned on four sides, about 8 minutes per batch. As each batch cooks, remove it from the pot with a slotted spoon and put in a bowl.

3. When all the pork is browned, pour off and discard all the fat from the pot. Return the pork to the pot and add 5 cups of stock, the palm sugar, soy sauce, dark soy sauce, oyster sauce, garlic and pepper.

4. Make a bouquet garni by wrapping the cilantro stems, cloves, star anise, cinnamon, coriander seeds and Sichuan peppercorns (if using) in a piece of cheesecloth and tying the four corners together. Add the bouquet garni to the pot.

5. Bring to a boil over medium-high heat. Reduce the heat to low and simmer, partially covered, until the pork is fork tender, 1½ to 2 hours. If needed, add water or more stock to keep the pork mostly submerged.

6. While the soup cooks, make medium-boiled eggs: Choose a pot large enough that the eggs will not be crowded (cook in batches, if necessary). Add water to come at least 1 inch above the eggs but don't add the eggs yet. Bring the water to a full, rolling boil over high heat, then, using a slotted spoon, slowly lower the eggs into the water. Boil for 8 minutes.

7. Meanwhile, pour cold water into a large bowl. When cooked, remove the eggs with the slotted spoon and place them in the cold water.

8. When the eggs are cool enough to handle, peel them carefully (the yolks will still be soft). If the eggs are difficult to peel, holding the eggs under running cold water as you peel them will help loosen the shells.

9. When the pork is fork tender, fish out and discard the bouquet garni. Add the peeled boiled eggs and the tofu puffs to the pot. Simmer gently for 8 more minutes. Remove the pot from the heat, taste, and adjust the seasoning with more salt if necessary. Remember that this soup is to be served over rice, so it should be strongly seasoned on its own.

10. If possible, let the soup sit for at least a few hours or overnight in the refrigerator before serving to let the eggs further absorb the flavor. Reheat gently over medium heat before serving.

11. Spoon the rice into warm bowls, then ladle the soup over the top. Garnish the soup with chopped cilantro.

This recipe is adapted from Hot Thai Kitchen *(Appetite by Random House, 2016).*

This soup is one of those better-the-next-day dishes. Traditionally, the eggs are simmered in the soup for at least 30 minutes so they absorb the flavors of the broth and the egg whites become very firm. I prefer more tender whites, so I like to make it the day before and let the eggs absorb the flavor without being cooked.

white bean, cabbage and sausage soup

Laura Keogh and Ceri Marsh
Cookbook Authors and Bloggers, sweetpotatochronicles.com

Like most soups, this one is made perfect by an afternoon of gentle simmering. We like to imagine this kind of afternoon, where our kids are getting along while they play board games, we get to (sigh) read a book, and family life is a hum of peaceable happiness. In reality, this scene almost never plays out. There are few open afternoons of quiet laziness and even less time for cooking. Luckily, this soup tastes almost as perfect when you've only got 30 minutes to throw it together. It's hearty without being heavy, is deeply satisfying and, along with a piece of bread, is dinner in a bowl. And that's just about as perfect as it gets.

Makes about 6 servings

2 Tbsp olive oil

3 Italian sausages, cut into bite-size pieces

1 onion, finely chopped

3 cloves garlic, minced

½ savoy or green cabbage, cored and thinly shredded (4 to 5 cups)

4 cups chicken stock

1 can (15 oz) cannellini beans, drained and rinsed

1 Tbsp fresh thyme leaves

2 bay leaves

Salt and pepper to taste

½ cup freshly grated Parmesan cheese

1. In a large pot, heat the oil over medium heat. Add the sausages and allow them to brown, pushing them around so they get color all over. Remove the sausages from the pot and set aside on a clean plate.

2. Add the onion and garlic to the pot and cook, stirring often, until the onion starts to soften, about 4 minutes. Add the cabbage and stir it around for a couple of minutes.

3. Add the stock, beans, thyme and bay leaves. Return the sausages to the pot and allow everything to come to a simmer over medium heat. Reduce the heat to medium-low and simmer, uncovered, until the vegetables are tender, about 20 minutes. Fish out and discard the bay leaves. Season with salt and pepper to taste.

4. Ladle the soup into warm bowls and serve with a generous sprinkling of Parmesan cheese.

nacho chicken soup

Barb Finley
Teacher, Chef and Founder of Project CHEF, Vancouver, BC

Gluten free

This is a recipe we use in the Project CHEF Summer Cooking Camps. Full of the flavors of Mexico, it is a big hit with the young chefs that create then gobble it up.

Makes about 4 servings

You can use either boneless or bone-in chicken thighs for this recipe. Just be sure to discard the bones before shredding the meat in step 4 if you opt for bone-in.

Omit the tortilla chips, or use gluten-free tortilla chips, to make this gluten free.

soup
2 Tbsp vegetable or olive oil
1 small onion, chopped
1 garlic clove, minced
2 Tbsp chili powder, or to taste
2 Tbsp tomato paste
4 skinless chicken thighs
Pinch of salt and pepper to taste
4 cups chicken stock (approx.)
6 cilantro stems
1 bay leaf

toppings (choose any or all)
1 cup fresh or frozen corn kernels
1 cup drained and rinsed canned black beans
1 Roma tomato, chopped
1 cup tortilla chips
½ cup crumbled feta or shredded Monterey Jack cheese
1 avocado, peeled, pitted and chopped
Cilantro leaves, torn
1 lime, cut into wedges

1. Heat the oil in a large pot over medium-low heat. Add the onion and garlic and cook, stirring often, until the onion is starting to soften, about 4 minutes. Add the chili powder and tomato paste and cook, stirring, for 1 minute. Add the chicken thighs to the pot and stir to coat them with the onion mixture. Season with a good pinch each of salt and pepper.

2. Add the stock, cilantro stems and bay leaf and bring to a boil over medium-high heat. Reduce the heat to medium-low and simmer, covered and stirring occasionally, until the chicken is tender and no longer pink inside, about 30 minutes, turning the chicken over after 15 minutes.

3. Using tongs, remove the chicken from the pot and place on a plate to cool. Fish out and discard the cilantro stems and bay leaf from the soup. While the chicken is cooling, get the toppings ready and put them all in individual bowls. Squeeze one of the lime wedges over the avocado to stop it from turning brown.

4. Once the chicken is cool enough to handle, shred it into bite-size pieces.

5. Place some shredded chicken in each soup bowl. Top the chicken with some corn, black beans and tomato. Ladle the soup into the bowls, then have everyone top their serving with tortilla chips, cheese, avocado, cilantro and a squeeze of lime.

new orleans crab and chicken gumbo

Christopher Ekpiken
Age 15, Runner-up on Food Network's Rachael Ray's Kids Cook-Off,
and YouTuber, youtube.com/chriswithatwist, Ann Arbor, MI

This soup is spicy and delicious and will warm you during the frigid winter months.

Makes about 8 servings

2 lb boneless, skinless chicken thighs	1 can (14 oz) diced tomatoes
Salt and pepper to taste	1 sweet green pepper, seeded and
2 Tbsp olive oil	chopped
½ cup butter	1 cup finely chopped green onions
12 oz andouille sausage, sliced (see	1 stalk celery, finely chopped
sidebar)	2 Tbsp Worcestershire sauce
1 large onion, finely chopped	1 Tbsp filé powder (see sidebar)
½ cup all-purpose flour	3 bay leaves
6 cups chicken stock	Cooked rice for serving
2 cups cooked crabmeat	Handful of finely chopped parsley

Andouille sausage is a smoked sausage popular in Louisiana. Specialty butcher stores often have it, but if you can't find it, kielbasa would be a good substitute.

1. Slice the chicken and season with salt and pepper to taste. In a large pot, heat the oil over medium heat. Add the chicken and cook until browned on all sides, about 8 minutes. Remove from the pot and set aside for later. Drain off the excess fat from the pot.

2. Add the butter to the pot and melt over medium heat. Add the andouille sausage and cook, stirring often, until the sausage is starting to brown, about 2 minutes. Add the onion and cook, stirring often, for 2 more minutes. Reduce the heat to low and cook, stirring occasionally, until the onion is softened, about 4 minutes.

3. In a small bowl, whisk together 1½ cups of warm water and the flour until smooth and creamy. Add the flour mixture to the pot, along with the browned chicken.

4. Add the stock, crabmeat, tomatoes (with their juices), green pepper, green onions, celery, Worcestershire sauce, filé powder and bay leaves. Bring to a boil over medium-high heat and boil, stirring often, for 10 minutes.

5. Reduce the heat to medium-low and simmer, covered, until the vegetables are tender and the chicken is no longer pink inside, about 40 minutes. Fish out and discard the bay leaves.

6. Spoon the rice into warm bowls, then ladle the soup over the top. Sprinkle with parsley and eat!

Filé powder is made from the ground young leaves and stems of the sassafras tree. It's used as a thickener and flavoring (it tastes a bit like root beer) in Creole and Cajun cooking. Look for it in specialty grocery stores or buy online.

maritime fish chowder

Laura Calder
Cookbook Author and TV Personality

This regional recipe comes from my mother and remains a staple in my own repertoire. It's easy, inexpensive, comforting and nutritious—and is forever a tie that binds me to home.

Makes about 8 servings

4 cups water
2½ lb frozen haddock (or a combination of cod and haddock)
4 lb Yukon Gold potatoes, peeled and finely chopped
2 large onions, finely chopped
1 can (12 oz) evaporated milk
1 cup half-and-half cream (10% MF) or whole milk (3.25% MF)
Salt and pepper to taste
Handful of finely chopped parsley
Sweet paprika to taste

1. In a large pot, combine the water and fish. Cover the pot and bring to a simmer over medium-low heat, simmering until the fish flakes, 15 to 20 minutes. Using a slotted spoon, remove the fish from the pot and set aside for later.

2. Increase the heat to medium and add the potatoes and onions to the fish broth. Simmer, covered, until the potatoes and onions are tender, about 20 minutes.

3. While the vegetables cook, flake the fish with a fork.

4. When the vegetables are tender, remove the pot from the heat and put the fish back in, along with the evaporated milk and half-and-half cream. Season with salt and pepper to taste, then stir in the parsley and paprika.

5. Ladle the soup into warm bowls or, for an even richer flavor, cool the soup completely, refrigerate it, then reheat the next day.

smoked salmon chowder

Lisa Ahier
Cookbook Author and Chef and Owner, SoBo, Tofino, BC

Canned chipotle peppers are smoked jalapeños packed in a pungent sauce. They add heat and lovely smoky flavor to all kinds of dishes. Although you only need 1 Tbsp of chipotle purée for this soup, it makes sense to purée the whole can. Spoon the remainder into a small container, seal and refrigerate for up to 4 days, or spoon into a small freezer bag, flatten to expel the air and freeze for several months. To use the frozen purée, simply break off the amount you need from the flattened pack.

When we first opened the SoBo food truck in Tofino, everyone and their brother in town made a clam chowder—except us. At least 20 times a day we'd get customers ordering chowder, but I resisted until one day the request came from my husband Artie's mother when she was visiting from New Brunswick. "Why would you not have chowder, dear? Everyone loves a good chowder!" I reluctantly took her advice, but just to be different I used smoked and fresh salmon rather than clams. The chowder is still on the menu and probably the most popular item we offer—proof that sometimes a mother does indeed know best!

Makes about 6 servings

6 Tbsp canola oil, divided
3 large onions, chopped and divided
3 large carrots, peeled and chopped
6 stalks celery, chopped
4 cups fish stock
1 lb potatoes, peeled and cubed
2 Tbsp dried oregano leaves
1 Tbsp dried basil leaves
1 Tbsp dried thyme leaves
1 Tbsp salt
3 cups whipping cream (35% MF)
1 lb boneless, skinless smoked salmon, coarsely chopped
½ cup roasted garlic cloves (recipe opposite)
1 small roasted sweet red pepper, stemmed and seeded (see page 115)
1 can (7 oz) chipotle chilies in adobo sauce (see sidebar)
1 lb boneless, skinless fresh salmon, cut into bite-size chunks
1 Tbsp finely chopped fresh dill

1. In a large, heavy-bottomed pot, heat 4 Tbsp of the oil over medium heat. Set aside 2 Tbsp of the chopped onions for later and add the remaining onions to the pot, along with the carrots and celery. Cook, stirring often, until the vegetables are tender, about 25 minutes.

2. Add the stock, potatoes, oregano, basil, thyme and salt and bring to a boil over

medium-high heat. Reduce the heat to medium-low and simmer, uncovered, until the potatoes are tender, about 20 minutes. Remove the pot from the heat and add the cream and the smoked salmon to the soup.

3. Meanwhile, put the garlic and roasted pepper in a food processor, then process until a smooth purée forms. Scrape the garlic-pepper purée into the soup.

4. Tip the can of chipotles into the food processor, then process until a smooth purée forms.

5. In a medium skillet, heat the remaining oil over medium-high heat. Add the fresh salmon, the remaining 2 Tbsp of onion and 1 Tbsp of the chipotle purée (see sidebar for how to store the remaining purée). Cook, stirring often, until the onion starts to soften and the chipotle purée coats the ingredients, 4 to 5 minutes.

6. Scrape the contents of the skillet into the soup pot and return it to medium heat. Simmer until the fresh salmon is just cooked and the chowder is hot throughout, about 5 minutes.

7. Ladle the soup into warm bowls and finish with a flourish of dill.

This recipe is adapted from The SOBO Cookbook *(Appetite by Random House, 2014).*

roasted garlic

1 whole head garlic
Olive oil
Salt and pepper to taste

1. Cut a slice from the top of the garlic head. Drizzle the exposed cloves with a little olive oil and sprinkle with salt and pepper to taste.

2. Wrap the head of garlic, along with an ice cube, in heavy duty foil. Roast on the barbecue over indirect medium heat, or in a 350°F oven, until nice and soft, about 30 minutes on the barbecue or 45 minutes in the oven. When the garlic is cool enough to handle, squeeze the cloves out of the skin, discarding the skin.

cabbage roll soup

Anna Olson
Chef, Cookbook Author and TV Personality

This recipe has all the key elements and great flavor of cabbage rolls, without the work of rolling and filling the cabbage leaves. As a kid, I loved my grandmother's cabbage rolls, but they were always a special occasion dish because of the work behind them. This soup takes the labor out of the process, but not the love!

Makes about 8 servings

3 slices bacon, finely chopped
1 medium onion, finely chopped
1 stalk celery, finely chopped
1 medium carrot, peeled and coarsely grated
1 lb ground beef or pork
1 clove garlic, minced
6 cups finely chopped green or savoy cabbage
2 cans (each 28 oz) diced tomatoes

2 cups chicken stock or water
½ cup long-grain brown rice (such as basmati)
¼ cup cider vinegar
2 Tbsp prepared horseradish
1 Tbsp paprika
2 tsp celery salt
2 bay leaves
Salt and pepper to taste
Sour cream for garnish

Like most stewy soups, this recipe tastes best reheated the next day, so get the kids in the kitchen with you to make it over the weekend and you've got dinner looked after during a busy week of homework, ballet and hockey practice.

The rice and cabbage keep absorbing liquid as the soup sits, so you may have to add a little water when you reheat it.

1. In a large, heavy-bottomed pot, cook the bacon over medium-high heat, stirring often, until it is crisp, 5 to 7 minutes. Using a slotted spoon, remove the bacon and drain it on a paper-towel-lined plate. Drain off all but 2 Tbsp of the fat in the pot.

2. Reduce the heat to medium. Add the onion, celery and carrot to the pot and cook, stirring often, until the onion is almost translucent, about 5 minutes.

3. Add the ground beef and cook, stirring often, until no longer pink, about 5 minutes. Add the garlic and cook, stirring, until it smells good, about 1 minute. Spoon off and discard any excess fat.

4. Add the cabbage, tomatoes (with their juices), stock, rice, vinegar, horseradish, paprika, celery salt and bay leaves and stir well. Cover the pot and bring it up to a full simmer. Reduce the heat to low and simmer, covered, until the rice is tender, about 40 minutes.

5. Fish out and discard the bay leaves. Add back the cooked bacon and season with salt and pepper to taste.

6. Ladle the soup into warm bowls and garnish each serving with a dollop of sour cream.

taco-seasoned chicken soup

Carson Wiebe
Age 12, Calgary, AB

I love Mexican food, so this soup is my perfect comfort food. My mom designed the recipe so it's unique.

Makes about 4 servings

Omit the tortilla chips, or use gluten-free tortilla chips, to make this gluten free.

soup
1⅓ lb boneless, skinless chicken breasts, finely chopped
Taco Seasoning (recipe opposite)
2 Tbsp avocado oil
1 large onion, finely chopped
4 large cloves garlic, minced
½ jalapeño, seeded and finely chopped
4 cups chicken stock
1 can (28 oz) diced tomatoes
1 can (19 oz) black beans, drained and rinsed

1 can (12 oz) corn kernels, drained
1 sweet yellow pepper, seeded and finely chopped
1 Tbsp lime juice
Salt to taste
Finely chopped cilantro for garnish

toppings
Shredded Monterey Jack cheese
Sour cream
Tortilla chips (your favorite kind)
Lime wedges

1. In a medium bowl, toss the finely chopped chicken in the taco seasoning to coat well.

2. In a large pot, heat the oil over medium heat. Add the onion, garlic and jalapeño. Cook, stirring often, until the onion has softened, about 8 minutes.

3. Add the seasoned chicken and cook, stirring often, until the chicken is no longer pink inside, 5 to 10 minutes.

4. Add the stock, tomatoes (with their juices), beans, corn, yellow pepper and lime juice. Bring to a simmer over medium heat. Season with salt to taste.

5. Ladle the soup into warm bowls and sprinkle each serving with cilantro. Serve with the toppings piled in separate bowls so everyone can help themselves to whatever they want on their soup.

taco seasoning

1 tsp chili powder

1 tsp each salt and pepper

¾ tsp ground cumin

¼ tsp dried oregano leaves

¼ tsp paprika

⅛ tsp garlic powder

⅛ tsp onion powder

⅛ tsp red chili flakes

1. In a small bowl, stir together all the ingredients.

zippy merguez tomato soup

Nicolas Latruwe
Age 12, Calgary, AB

This Moroccan-inspired soup with spicy merguez sausage packs a little punch.

For a silky smooth soup, pour it through a fine-mesh sieve set over a clean pot after blending or, if you don't mind tomato seeds in your soup, don't sieve it.

Makes about 6 servings

1 can (12 oz) tomato paste
12 oz merguez sausages
4 stalks celery, finely chopped
2 carrots, peeled and chopped
1 onion, finely chopped

6 cups vegetable stock
16 tomatoes, cored
2 cups couscous
Salt and pepper to taste
Finely chopped parsley for garnish

1. In a small skillet, cook the tomato paste over medium heat, stirring often, until it darkens, 4 to 5 minutes. Remove the skillet from the heat and set aside for later.

2. In a large pot, cook the merguez sausages, turning often, until browned and fully cooked, about 10 minutes. Add the celery, carrots and onion to the pot and cook, stirring often, until the onion has softened, about 8 minutes.

3. Add the stock and bring to a boil over medium-high heat. Reduce the heat to medium-low and simmer, partially covered, until the vegetables are tender, about 15 minutes.

4. Meanwhile, bring a large saucepan of water to a boil over high heat. With a small, sharp knife, cut the cores from the tomatoes. Add the tomatoes to the pot of boiling water and blanch for 10 to 20 seconds. Using a slotted spoon, remove the tomatoes from the pot. When the tomatoes are cool enough to handle, peel off the skins with a paring knife (the skin should come right off), then cut the tomatoes into quarters.

5. Using tongs, remove the sausages from the pot, put on a plate and set aside to cool slightly. Add the tomatoes and reserved tomato paste to the pot of soup. Bring the soup to a boil, then remove from the heat.

6. Using an immersion blender in the pot, blend the soup until smooth.

7. Cut the merguez sausages into bite-size pieces and add to the soup, along with the couscous. Bring to a simmer over medium heat and simmer, uncovered, until the couscous is tender, about 5 minutes. Season the soup with salt and pepper to taste.

8. Ladle the soup into warm bowls and scatter each spicy bowlful with parsley.

baka's beef soup

Mario and Klaudia Mihaljevic
Ages 9 and 7, Calgary, AB

We like this soup because it tastes and smells really good and is easy to make. Our mama and baka make it for us when our tummies are upset and it makes us feel better. Our mama used to eat it when she was our age!

Makes about 4 servings

6 cups lukewarm water
1 to 2 lb bone-in beef brisket or beef shank, rinsed
6 cups cold water
3 stalks celery
2 large carrots, peeled
1 celery root, peeled
1 parsnip, peeled
1 onion, cut in half
½ cup whole black peppercorns
¼ cup salt
¼ cup tomato paste
1 cup fine egg noodles

The secret to the homemade broth is in the long cooking over low heat; this way, the flavors merge and the soup will not only taste richer but also have an attractive, golden color. The boiled beef is very flavorful and can be served on its own with horseradish and a fine loaf of bread.

1. In a large pot, combine the lukewarm water and beef and bring to a boil over medium-high heat.

2. Immediately drain the cooking water, then return the beef to the pot, along with the cold water, celery, carrots, celery root, parsnip, onion, peppercorns, salt and tomato paste.

3. Bring to a boil over medium-high heat. Reduce the heat to low and simmer, partially covered, until the beef is tender, about 90 minutes.

4. Remove the beef from the pot and set aside to cool slightly. Strain the broth, discarding all the vegetables and flavorings, except the carrots. Return the broth and the carrots to the pot.

5. When the beef is cool enough to handle, cut it into bite-size pieces, discarding the bone. Set aside (see sidebar).

6. Bring the soup back to a simmer, then add the egg noodles. Simmer, uncovered, until the noodles are tender, about 5 minutes. Ladle into warm bowls and enjoy!

thai coconut curry shrimp soup

Emilia Augello
Age 16, first ever *Chopped Canada* Teen Tournament Champion, 2015, Montreal, QC

I like this soup because I love the fragrant flavors of Thai food, one of my favorite cuisines.

Makes about 4 servings

1 Tbsp sesame oil
4 cloves garlic, minced
2 tsp minced fresh ginger
4 cups chicken stock
2 cups coconut milk
Grated zest and squeezed juice of
  2 limes
Grated zest of 1 lemon
4 tsp soy sauce
3 tsp mirin (see sidebar)
1 tsp curry powder

1 tsp black pepper
½ tsp white pepper
½ tsp cayenne (optional)
½ tsp salt
½ tsp fish sauce
36 large raw shrimp, peeled and
  deveined
2 carrots, peeled and grated
2 handfuls of coarsely chopped cilantro,
  divided
4 green onions, sliced

Mirin is a sweet Japanese rice wine. In the soup, the alcohol is simmered off during cooking, making it okay to serve to kids.

1. In a large pot, heat the oil over high heat. Add the garlic and ginger and cook, stirring, until they are slightly browned, about 2 minutes.

2. Add the stock and coconut milk and bring to a boil. Reduce the heat to medium and simmer for 5 minutes.

3. Meanwhile, whisk together the lime zest and juice, lemon zest, soy sauce, mirin, curry powder, black pepper, white pepper, cayenne (if using), salt and fish sauce in a small bowl. Add the mixture into the pot and stir well.

4. Add the shrimp and carrots and simmer, stirring occasionally, until the shrimp are pink and firm and the carrots are tender, 3 to 4 minutes.

5. Taste for seasonings, adding more salt or soy sauce, if desired, and more cayenne for those who like it spicy. Stir in half of the cilantro.

6. Ladle the soup into warm bowls and top each serving with the green onions and remaining cilantro. Enjoy!

cheeseburger soup

Liam Lewis
Age 15, Little Locavore Blogger, thelittlelocavore.ca, Vancouver, BC

My parents would "hide" nutrition inside my favorite foods like this cheeseburger soup. Cauliflower is a very stealthy vegetable that can sneak into many delicious meals, and their baked macaroni and cheese almost always had a hidden head of cauliflower inside. After I started cooking, my parents let me in on their secrets to make my "picky eater" plates healthier.

Makes about 4 servings

3 Tbsp butter
¼ cup finely chopped shallots
2 cloves garlic, minced
3 cups chopped cauliflower florets
½ sweet red pepper, seeded and
  chopped
3 Tbsp all-purpose flour

3 cups beef stock
2 tsp your favorite mustard
2 cups shredded old white cheddar
  cheese
1 lb extra-lean ground beef
Salt and pepper to taste
Cheeseburger toppings (see sidebar)

1. In a large pot, melt the butter over medium heat. Add the shallots and garlic and cook, stirring often, until the shallots start to soften, 3 to 5 minutes.

2. Add the cauliflower and red pepper and cook, stirring, until the red pepper is tender, about 5 minutes.

3. Add the flour and stir until well blended. Immediately add the stock and mustard, stirring well to combine. Bring to a boil over medium-high heat, stirring constantly. Reduce the heat to medium-low and simmer, uncovered and stirring occasionally, until the cauliflower is tender, about 15 minutes.

4. Add the cheese, ¼ cup at a time, stirring until each addition is melted before adding more. Remove the pot from the heat and set aside.

5. In a large skillet over medium-high heat, cook the beef, seasoning it with salt and pepper to taste and stirring, until no longer pink, about 8 minutes. You can break up the larger lumps with the spoon or leave it chunkier. Drain off and discard the excess fat, then set aside.

6. Using an immersion blender in the pot, blend the soup until smooth. Stir in the cooked beef. Reheat the soup gently over medium heat.

7. Ladle the soup into warm bowls and garnish with your favorite cheeseburger toppings (see sidebar).

Prefer a chunkier soup? Skip the puréeing step.

Choose your favorite cheeseburger toppings to garnish this soup:
• Chopped chives
• Sliced tomatoes (cherry are best, because they are bite-size small)
• Pickle slices
• More cheese (please!)
• Ketchup or mustard drizzle
• Red chili flakes or hot pepper sauce to taste

For a gluten-free soup, replace the flour with 1½ Tbsp cornstarch, whisking it with about ½ cup cold stock before adding it to the pot.

For a vegetarian soup, use vegetable stock and replace the ground beef with your favorite vegetable protein.

butter chicken chowder

Madeline Dunn
Age 11, Calgary, AB

I am really starting to like Indian food. My mom is a chef and culinary arts teacher, so we created this recipe for her school to use in its café.

Makes about 4 servings

1 cup finely chopped onion
3 Tbsp vegetable oil, divided
2 Tbsp lime juice
1 Tbsp minced fresh ginger
1 Tbsp paprika
1 Tbsp chili powder
2 cloves garlic, minced
1 tsp garam masala (see page 34)
1 tsp salt
Pinch of cayenne
Pinch of ground nutmeg
5 boneless, skinless chicken thighs, cut into pieces
Salt and pepper to taste
¼ cup butter
¼ cup tomato paste
3 cups chicken stock, plus more if necessary
1 Tbsp packed brown sugar
⅓ cup crushed cashew nuts
1¼ cups cubed, cooked waxy potatoes
1¼ cups frozen peas, thawed and drained
¾ cup whipping cream (35% MF)
Plain yogurt for garnish
Finely chopped cilantro for garnish
Toasted naan bread to serve (optional)

1. In a food processor, make a wet masala by combining the onion, 1 Tbsp of the oil, the lime juice, ginger, paprika, chili powder, garlic, garam masala, salt, cayenne and nutmeg. Pulse until the mixture is finely minced and fairly smooth. Scrape the wet masala out of the food processor and set aside in a small bowl.

2. Sprinkle the chicken with salt and pepper to taste. In a large pot, heat the remaining oil over medium heat. Cooking in batches so as not to crowd the pot, cook the chicken until browned on all sides, about 8 minutes per batch. As each batch browns, remove it from the pot with a slotted spoon and put in a bowl.

3. When all the chicken is browned, drain off as much of the fat as possible from the pot. Melt the butter in the pot. Add the wet masala and cook, stirring often, for 5 minutes. Add the tomato paste and cook, stirring, for 2 to 3 minutes.

4. Add the stock and brown sugar and bring to a boil over medium-high heat. Reduce the heat to medium and simmer for 10 minutes.

5. Return the chicken to the pot, along with any juices in the bowl. Add the cashews. Simmer, uncovered and stirring occasionally, for 20 minutes. If the soup is too thick, add a little more stock.

6. Add the potatoes, peas and cream. Reduce the heat to low and simmer for 5 minutes.

7. Ladle the soup into warm bowls and top with a dollop of yogurt and a scattering of cilantro. Serve with toasted naan bread, if you like.

crock-pot tortilla soup

Liam Minck
Age 11, Kelowna, BC

This soup tastes so good even my brother eats it.

Makes about 10 servings

4 cups chicken stock
4 chicken breasts (fresh or frozen)
1 can (28 oz) tomatoes (with their juices)
1 can (19 oz) lentils
1 can (19 oz) black beans
1 can (19 oz) navy or fava beans
1 can (4 oz) chilies
⅓ cup finely chopped cilantro
1 cup shredded cheddar cheese to garnish
Sour cream and tortilla chips to serve

Omit the tortilla chips, or use gluten-free tortilla chips, to make this gluten free.

1. Put all of the ingredients, except the cilantro, cheese, sour cream and tortilla chips, into a slow cooker. Turn the slow cooker to high and cook for 6 to 8 hours.

2. Using tongs, remove the chicken from the soup and set aside until it is cool enough to handle. Shred the chicken meat and return it to the soup. Stir well.

3. Ladle the soup into warm bowls and scatter each portion with cilantro. Serve topped with cheese, sour cream and tortilla chips.

cock-a-leekie soup with cheesy croutons

Michael Bonacini
Chef and TV Personality

This is one of the first soups we made in chef school. I remember it well, not just because it is hearty and delicious, but because the name made us all laugh, every time. What can I say? We were young and immature!

Makes about 6 servings

¼ cup vegetable oil
1 medium onion, finely chopped
1 clove garlic, minced
2½ cups cubed, peeled potatoes (about ¼-inch cubes)
1 large sprig thyme
6 cups chicken stock
3 cups chopped trimmed leeks (about ¾-inch pieces)
Salt and pepper to taste
1 boneless, skinless chicken breast or 1 cup cooked chicken meat
6 to 8 prunes, pitted and cut into strips
Cheesy Croutons (recipe follows)

1. In a large pot, heat the oil over medium heat. Add the onion and garlic and cook, stirring often, until the onion has softened, about 8 minutes.

2. Add the potatoes and thyme and continue to cook, stirring often, for an additional 2 to 3 minutes.

3. Add the stock, leeks and salt and pepper to taste. Bring to a simmer over medium heat, skimming off any foam that's risen to the surface. Simmer, uncovered, until the potatoes and leek are very tender, 30 to 40 minutes.

4. If using a boneless, skinless chicken breast, add it to the pot and continue simmering gently until the chicken breast is no longer pink inside, about 15 minutes.

5. Using tongs, remove the chicken breast and set aside until cool enough to handle.

6. Divide the prunes among the soup bowls. Shred the chicken breast and add to the prunes in the bowls. (If using cooked chicken meat, add it now.)

This is a soup that was traditionally served in Scotland, although the cheesy croutons are my personal addition. If I'm feeling extravagant, Stilton is my preferred choice of cheese. A bowl of this soup in the fall with a crusty piece of bread is simply delicious!

Omit the croutons for a gluten-free soup.

Remember soups made a day ahead always taste best.

7. Fish out and discard the thyme sprig from the soup. Taste the soup and adjust the seasonings if necessary. Ladle the soup into the bowls, scatter with cheesy croutons and serve at once.

cheesy croutons

3 slices crusty bread
1 Tbsp Dijon mustard
1 cup shredded cheddar cheese

1. Preheat the broiler to high. Brush the bread slices on both sides with mustard.
2. Broil one side of the bread until nicely toasted. Once toasted, flip the bread over and sprinkle cheese on the untoasted side of the bread slices, then broil, cheese side up, until the cheese has melted.
3. Roughly cut each slice into crouton-size pieces and use to garnish any soup.

sausage sauce soup

Rosie Daykin
Cookbook Author and Owner, Butter Baked Goods, Vancouver, BC

Growing up, my daughter India's favorite meal was pasta with something we like to call sausage sauce. Now 24, she still asks me to make that dish on her birthday. I thought it might be fun to combine all those same elements to create a delicious and hearty soup.

Makes about 6 servings

3 mild Italian sausages, cut into ½-inch pieces
4 slices thick-cut bacon, cut into ½-inch pieces
4 cups chicken stock
1 can (28 oz) whole tomatoes
1 cup drained and rinsed canned chickpeas
½ cup orzo pasta
3 Tbsp butter
1 Tbsp balsamic vinegar
¼ tsp each salt and pepper
¼ cup finely chopped fresh basil
Freshly grated Parmesan cheese
Rustic bread to serve

1. In a large pot over medium-high heat, combine the sausages and bacon. Cook, stirring often, until the bacon is just starting to get a little crispy and the sausage pieces are cooked through, 10 to 15 minutes.

2. Remove the pot from the heat and tilt it to one side to allow the excess fat to pool. Use a large spoon to spoon off and discard the fat.

3. Add the stock and tomatoes (with their juices) to the pot. Bring to a boil over high heat, using the back of a large spoon to help break the tomatoes down into smaller chunks.

4. Add the chickpeas, orzo, butter, balsamic vinegar and salt and pepper. Reduce the heat to medium-low and simmer, covered, until the orzo is tender, about 15 minutes. Add the basil and give the soup a stir.

5. Ladle the soup into warm bowls and serve with a generous sprinkle of grated Parmesan on top and some nice chewy bread alongside.

chill out

NOT ALL SOUP NEEDS TO BE HOT. FOR SOMETHING VERY DIFFERENT, try a chilled soup. An icy bowlful is so refreshing to sip on a steamy summer's day—especially when it's too hot to cook. This chapter features several soups created to be eaten cold. Some are savory, some are sweet, but all are best when they're chilling out.

Mary's Cold Cherry Soup (page 195)

roasted okanagan tomato gazpacho

Jennifer Schell
Soup Sister, Cookbook Author and Editor, *Food & Wine Trails*

This recipe is a celebration of summertime in the Okanagan, starring the beloved tomato. Almost all of the ingredients can be found at the local farmers' market, so take the kids along for the shop to experience sourcing direct from the farmers. My friend the chef Vincent Denis shared this recipe in my latest cookbook.

Makes about 4 servings

2 lb ripe tomatoes
2 Tbsp olive oil
½ cup seeded and chopped sweet red pepper
½ cup cored, chopped fennel
½ cup peeled, seeded and chopped cucumber
½ cup chopped red onion
2 Tbsp apple cider vinegar

2 Tbsp Worcestershire sauce
1 medium jalapeño, seeded and finely chopped
2 cloves garlic, minced
1 tsp salt
½ tsp pepper
½ tsp ground cumin
2 Tbsp finely slivered fresh basil leaves for garnish

Cold soup will be a new idea for many young palates so serve with a shoal of goldfish crackers floating on top for an added enticement to taste.

1. Preheat the oven to 450°F. Cut out the cores from the tomatoes and place the tomatoes in a single layer in a shallow roasting pan. Drizzle with the olive oil. Roast, uncovered, until the skins loosen and turn brown, 15 to 20 minutes. Remove from the oven and set aside to cool.

2. When the tomatoes are cool enough to handle, peel off the skins and chop the tomatoes coarsely.

3. In a very large bowl, toss the tomatoes with the red pepper, fennel, cucumber, onion, vinegar, Worcestershire sauce, jalapeño, garlic, salt, pepper and cumin.

4. Working in batches, process the tomato mixture in a blender on high speed until smooth, tipping each blended batch into a second very large bowl. Chill the soup until ready to serve.

5. Ladle the soup into chilled bowls and serve with a drift of slivered basil over each portion.

This recipe is adapted from The Butcher, The Baker, The Wine & Cheese Maker in the Okanagan *by Jennifer Schell (TouchWood Editions, 2016).*

chilled leek and potato soup (vichyssoise)

Mardi Michels
Food Blogger, eatlivetravelwrite.com

This easy soup is wonderful cold (as it was intended to be served), or hot if the weather is chilly—it's a soup for any season. Because the soup is blended until it's smooth, the chopping of the vegetables doesn't have to be precise, making it ideal for novice cooks. You don't have to peel the potatoes if you don't want to, but it does result in a smoother soup. The creaminess comes from the addition of Greek yogurt when it's served, not cream, so it's a lighter version of the classic.

Makes about 4 servings

2 Tbsp olive oil
2 Tbsp butter
1 large onion, thinly sliced
4 small leeks (white and light green parts only), thinly sliced
4 cups vegetable or chicken stock
4 medium potatoes, peeled and chopped into 1-inch cubes
Salt and pepper to taste
Plain Greek yogurt for garnish, about 1 Tbsp per serving
Chopped chives for garnish

1. In a large heavy-bottomed pot, heat the oil and butter over medium-high heat. Add the onion and cook, stirring often, until it begins to soften but not color, about 5 minutes.

2. Add the leeks and stir to thoroughly coat them with the butter and oil. Continue to cook, stirring often, until the leeks are softened, about 5 more minutes.

3. Add the stock and potatoes and bring to a boil over high heat. Reduce the heat to medium-low and simmer, uncovered, until the potatoes are very soft (they should mash easily with a fork), about 20 minutes.

4. Remove the pot from the heat and allow the soup to cool. Using an immersion blender in the pot, blend the soup until smooth. Refrigerate the soup until chilled or reheat it over medium heat. Season with salt and pepper to taste.

5. Ladle the soup into bowls and serve warm or chilled. Either way, top each serving with a dollop of plain Greek yogurt and a sprinkle of chives.

It's not entirely clear who came up with this soup, but most credit the French chef Louis Diat, who was working at the Ritz Carlton Hotel in New York in 1917. It's said that Diat created a leek and potato soup that he remembered from his childhood growing up near Vichy in France, but cooled it down with milk to serve on the hotel's rooftop patio. He served it chilled and called it *Crème Vichyssoise*.

grandma jackie's andalusian gazpacho

Malcolm Knapp-Durante
Age 14, Calgary, AB

I got this recipe from my grandmother. She lives in Spain and this is a Spanish soup. It's easy to make because you don't have to cook it. You just cut stuff up or buy it already cut up. You eat it cold so it's good for the summer. It is very popular in Spain and sometimes they add cream and croutons. You can eat it blended or chunky—I like it chunky.

Makes about 8 servings

1 can (48 oz) tomato juice
3 cups cored and finely chopped tomatoes
1 sweet yellow pepper, seeded and finely chopped
1 cucumber, peeled and finely chopped
1 cup finely chopped sweet onion
3 green onions, finely chopped
1 tsp minced garlic
1 lemon
1 lime
¼ cup finely chopped parsley
1 Tbsp finely chopped fresh basil
1 tsp sweet smoked paprika
Salt and pepper to taste

1. Pour the tomato juice into a very large bowl. Add the tomatoes, yellow pepper, cucumber, sweet onion, green onions and garlic.

2. Cut the lemon and the lime in half and squeeze the juice into the bowl.

3. Stir in the parsley, basil, smoked paprika and salt and pepper to taste. Refrigerate the soup until it is chilled.

4. Ladle the soup into chilled bowls and dive in!

chilled tomato soup with mozzarella-grape crostini

Claudio Aprile
Chef and Owner, Origin Restaurant & Bar, Toronto, ON

This soup is almost more fun to make than it is to eat. Our kids really enjoy seeing how all these garden vegetables can be transformed into a bright yellow soup that's packed with nutritious ingredients. I love teaching my kids how eating healthy can be so much fun—it's a win-win for me.

Makes 8 servings

tomato soup
½ cup warm, unseasoned rice wine
    vinegar
1 tsp saffron threads
8 cups cored and chopped yellow
    tomatoes
1 cup peeled, cored and chopped
    Asian pear
1 cup chopped celery
1 cup seeded and chopped
    sweet yellow pepper
1 cup peeled, chopped cucumber
½ cup cored, chopped fennel
½ cup chopped shallots
½ cup olive oil (preferably extra virgin)

Grated zest and squeezed juice of
    1 lemon
10 Thai basil leaves, chopped
1 tsp finely chopped garlic
½ tsp smoked paprika
Salt to taste

almond milk (see sidebar)
1 cup blanched almonds
1 cup mineral water
Salt to taste

Extra virgin olive oil for drizzling
Grape and Mozzarella Crostini (recipe
    follows)

If you don't want to make your own almond milk, substitute any unsweetened almond milk.

1. For the tomato soup, put the warm rice vinegar in a small bowl and sprinkle the saffron over the surface. Set aside to soak for 10 minutes.

2. Tip the saffron mixture into a very large bowl and add the tomatoes, Asian pear, celery, yellow pepper, cucumber, fennel, shallots, oil, lemon zest and juice, basil, garlic, paprika and salt to taste. Toss the ingredients until well combined.

3. Working in batches, process the tomato mixture in a food processor on high speed until smooth, tipping each processed batch through a fine-mesh sieve into a second very large bowl. Chill the soup until ready to serve.

4. For the almond milk, place the almonds, water and salt into a blender or the rinsed-out food processor. Blend on high speed until smooth. Strain through a clean fine-mesh sieve and chill until ready to serve.

5. Ladle the soup into eight chilled bowls. Drizzle 2 Tbsp of the almond milk on top of each portion of soup, then drizzle with a little extra virgin olive oil. Serve the crostini on the side (recipe follows).

grape and mozzarella crostini

Omit the crostini to make this soup gluten-free.

Makes 8 crostini

8 slices pumpernickel bread, each 2- x 1- x ½-inch
2 Tbsp olive oil
2 balls bocconcini cheese
12 seedless green grapes, cut in half
8 sprigs watercress
Salt to taste

1. Preheat the oven to 350°F.
2. Brush the bread slices with olive oil and arrange on a rimmed baking sheet. Bake for 5 minutes or until crisp. Remove the bread from the oven.
3. Cut each bocconcini ball into four equal slices. Place one slice of cheese onto each crostini and top evenly with grapes. Garnish each crostini with a watercress sprig and sprinkle with salt to taste.

icy raspberry-yogurt soup

Matthew Batey and Charlotte Batey
Executive Chef, The Nash, and daughter, Calgary, AB

My 6-year-old daughter Charlotte is a great helper in the kitchen; some days you'd
swear she is the chef! This is a simple recipe that she can make on her own with
minimal supervision. A little help with the blender and she is creating herself a
tasty, nutritious soup that can be served cold or frozen into Popsicles for a hot
summer day (see sidebar).

Makes about 8 servings

4 cups fresh raspberries
2 Tbsp local honey or more to taste
¼ cup raspberry juice (or apple, if you can't find raspberry)
6 to 8 fresh mint leaves
1 cup cow- or goat-milk yogurt
Cold-pressed canola oil for drizzling (optional)

1. Place the raspberries, honey, juice and mint in a countertop blender. Ensure the
   lid is on securely.

2. Starting on low speed then increasing to high, blend the mixture until it is
   completely smooth.

3. Set a fine-mesh sieve over a large pitcher. Pour the raspberry mixture through
   the sieve to remove the raspberry seeds.

4. Whisk the yogurt into the soup and whisk in a little more honey, if you like it
   sweeter.

5. Pour the soup into chilled bowls and, for a nice nutty flavor, finish with a drizzle
   of cold-pressed canola oil, if you like.

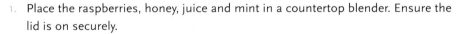

This soup makes a
yummy and healthy
dessert treat or snack
if you pour it into
Popsicle molds and
freeze it.

More yogurt and a
handful of fresh berries
makes a pretty garnish
for this soup.

the summer kiss

Logan Guleff
Age 15, MasterChef Junior Winner, Memphis, TN

I created this recipe for a fundraiser in Virginia when I was 12 years old. It was a hot summer event and I wanted something fresh, cool and aromatic. So I created a cold soup that screams summer: it highlights fresh ingredients and is really refreshing. I have also used it to make some fruity Popsicles.

Makes about 4 servings

2 Tbsp butter
4 cups peeled, pitted and sliced fresh peaches (see sidebar)
2 Tbsp brown sugar
½ small fennel bulb, cored and thinly sliced
1 cup Greek yogurt with honey
1 tsp fresh lemon juice
3 dashes hot pepper sauce
Pinch of salt
2 Tbsp rose water (see sidebar)
Edible flowers (optional)

1. In a large saucepan, melt the butter over medium heat. Add the peaches and sugar. Cook, stirring often, until the peaches are soft and the sugar has caramelized, about 5 to 7 minutes. Scrape the peach mixture into a countertop blender.

2. In the same saucepan, cook the fennel, stirring often, until it is soft and semi-translucent, about 10 minutes. Add the fennel to the blender.

3. Blend the peach-fennel mixture until smooth. Add the yogurt, lemon juice, hot pepper sauce and salt, then blend again until smooth. Pour the soup into a large pitcher and refrigerate until chilled.

4. Just before serving, stir in the rose water, then pour the soup into chilled bowls. Float edible flowers (if using) in each bowl.

Be sure to use fresh, ripe peaches in this recipe. If your peaches are very sweet, you may need less sugar.

Rose water is made by steeping rose petals in water and has an intense floral flavor. Look for it in larger supermarkets or natural food stores, making sure you buy culinary rose water that's safe to eat.

If you use soy yogurt, this soup is suitable for vegans; just adjust the sugar, adding about 1 Tbsp more.

mary's cold cherry soup

Kimberley Seldon
Design Editor of *Chatelaine* and TV Personality

This recipe is from my mum-in-law Mary Seldon's kitchen. Mary (or Granny as she's known) has six grandchildren and three great-grandchildren (and those numbers are rising rapidly). Her kitchen is a busy place. On warm summer nights this cold cherry soup is a kid fave (though grown-ups like it, too). Because it's vegetarian, my daughter Raleigh loves it too.

Makes about 4 to 6 servings

1 jar (24 oz) pitted sour red cherries
½ tsp salt
1 Tbsp all-purpose flour
1 cup sour cream
Fresh mint leaves for garnish

1. Tip the contents of the jar of cherries into a large saucepan. Fill the empty cherry jar with water and add it to the saucepan, along with the salt.

2. Bring the cherry mixture to a rapid boil over high heat. Reduce the heat to low and simmer until the cherries are soft, about 5 minutes.

3. In a small bowl, whisk the flour with a little water to make a smooth paste, which will help thicken the soup. Add the flour paste to the boiling soup. Cook, stirring, until smooth.

4. Stir in the sour cream and remove the saucepan from the heat. Let the soup cool, then refrigerate until chilled.

5. Ladle the soup into chilled bowls and scatter with fresh mint leaves.

Because it is served cold, it is safe to let children ladle the soup into the bowls, but be aware the cherries may stain clothing and upholstery, so supervision is required.

creating a stir

A mere eight years ago, I had a little idea to create a philanthropic enterprise with soup making and soup-giving at its heart. Nearly 30 Soup Sisters chapters and two best-selling soup cookbooks later, I am deeply gratified and humbled at what thousands of volunteers have been able to achieve.

We now have chapters across Canada and we have begun to make our presence known in the US as well. Every month, in a local commercial kitchen, each Soup Sisters chapter gathers together dozens of paying volunteers for a fun, social evening of chopping and stirring. These community soup makers find us through word of mouth, their workplace, book club or other social networks. Our events are often booked months or up to a year in advance. Each event produces enough homemade soup to feed the residents of a local emergency shelter for an entire month, and we provide for the same shelters every month so that they can rely on our contribution. With this simple but compelling formula, more than 40,000 soup-making participants have helped us feed and nurture more than 100,000 women, children and youth each year since 2009.

The Soup Sisters experience is carefully designed to meet three important criteria:

- Hands-on participation in a social enterprise where everyone pays to volunteer to "do good."
- Production of a tangible product that will help people in the local community.
- Enjoyment of a memorable volunteer experience in a warm, familiar and nurturing setting where participants learn about the issue of domestic violence from a speaker from the recipient shelter.

Soup Sisters aims to create a uniquely safe, productive and happy space where everyone—regardless of gender, age, experience or comfort level—can join together to help those in their community suffering from family violence and the alienation that comes with it. For most people, this is a first. Family violence is a heavy, emotionally loaded and often uncomfortable issue that does not lend itself easily to volunteer opportunities.

But Soup Sisters events are filled with a joyful sense of kitchen camaraderie and common purpose that sees our volunteers return time and again to offer their good will and stirring skills. In this setting, an uncomfortable topic becomes accessible and safe to learn and talk about.

For the soup recipients—many of whom are in a precarious physical, emotional and financial state—the result is a very tangible affirmation that they are not forgotten. It is evidence that hundreds of local people are reaching out in an effort to comfort them, fill their stomachs and heal their souls—one made-from-scratch, nutritious bowl of soup at a time.

In purchasing this latest cookbook or either of the two other Soup Sisters books, you are contributing to our efforts to support families in crisis and assisting us in spreading greater awareness about domestic violence. In addition to our regular programming, we are always looking for other ways to help those in need, like our three-city Soup for Syrians Soup-a-Thon that we organized to welcome refugees to Canada, or our "Big Stir" team-building events.

For more about Soup Sisters and Broth Brothers, or to volunteer, please visit www.soupsisters.org.

introducing our souper kids

Please meet the wonderful, inspiring young chefs who contributed recipes to this book and are just starting to flex their culinary and charitable muscles.

Mrs. Foster's Grade 2 Class (page 121)
We are Mrs. Foster's Grade 2 class of 2015–2016 from Shannon Lake Elementary School in West Kelowna, BC. Most of us are 7 years old. Our class is very involved in planting, tending and harvesting our food garden at school. As we explored the food groups and learned how food gets to our plate, we became very interested in learning how to cook. After reading a story about a chubby king who wanted a cook who could create unusual recipes, we brainstormed and created Dragon Soup.

Lachlan Allemeier (page 95)
I am 13 years old and I love playing rugby and learning martial arts. I like to find out new things about food and cooking from my dad.

Emilia Augello (page 171)
I am 16 years old and absolutely passionate about cooking. When I am in the kitchen, I feel like I can be myself. I love Italian and Asian flavors and love creating my own recipes, and look forward to going to culinary school and traveling in the future. I enjoy cooking for others and feel proud when I hear they have enjoyed my dishes.

Charlotte Batey (page 191)
I am 6 years old and enjoy crafts, mud, catching frogs, singing and creating recipes from scratch. I call them "brain recipes." I enjoy my very large family, my friends and toys. My favorite foods include my grandpa's oatmeal, as well as my mama's homemade mac and cheese.

Annie Corrin (page 36)
I just finished Grade 3 and I like to play piano, do arts and crafts and I'm very good at tennis. I also love sleepover camp. One of my favorite things to make for my family is a dessert platter with fruit and chocolate sauce.

Simon Drever (page 71)
I play soccer a lot. I love my dog, Bear. I'm 12 years old and in Grade 6. I hope they find a cure for childhood cancer.

Madeline Dunn (page 175)
I am a Grade 7 student at Queen Elizabeth Junior High School in Calgary. I love to read, play with my two cats, Jack and Lily, and play on my computer. I belong to a figure skating club and play violin. I like to spend time in the kitchen with my parents, but I especially like to bake with my mom.

Christopher Ekpiken (page 159)
I am 15 years old, live in Ann Arbor, Michigan, and competed on Food Network's *Rachael Ray's Kids Cook-Off* TV series. When I was 6 years old, my mom found me in the kitchen at 4 a.m. preparing to bake a cake. When I cook, I often transform the original recipe into something fun, fresh and new—that's why people call me "Chris with a Twist." I'm also an avid gamer and recently started my own gaming web series.

Shamus Faulkner (page 62)
I am 12 years old and going into Grade 6. I care about my sister Elise. Also the homeless and ill. I realize how fortunate I am to have a home. My hobbies are swimming, golfing, playing rugby and eating the food I make.

Emily Grace (page 142)
I am a 17-year-old entrepreneur and I sell my sweet creations at local farmers' markets and stores in the Orlando area. A portion of every sale from my bake sales goes to a local charity called Give Kids the World. I have big dreams of becoming a world renowned pastry chef. I hope you enjoy my soup recipe as much as I do.

Taya Groner (page 68)
I am 9 years old. I love singing and writing my own songs, dancing, swimming and playing at the park or beach with my friends and my puppy, Koah. I really love my mom's homemade soups, which she has been making for me since I was a baby. I like helping her in the kitchen, especially when she bakes cookies or when she makes crêpes on Saturday mornings.

Logan Guleff (page 193)
I am 15 years old and live in Memphis, Tennessee, home of great barbecue and the blues. I have always loved to cook and won my first award when I was 8. When I am not cooking, I love to climb rock walls, build Lego and, of course, play video games. I love all kinds of technology and hope to be part of the team that develops sustainable food for the first manned mission to Mars.

Jesse Gunn (page 130)
I am 13 years old and started cooking when I was 10. I live in New York City where I am exposed to all kinds of exciting types of foods. I am a high honor student and my favorite subjects are math and science. I also play guitar and I am in two bands. My favorite things to cook are dim sum, soufflé, crème brûlée and a good steak.

Aston Hemming (page 67)
I am 6 years old and in Grade 2. I enjoy traveling with my family and trying new foods and adventures. I am a singer, dancer and actress and I love nature, the forest and birds. I like to use my imagination and I have a big sense of humor.

Sophie Henderson (page 111)
I am 17 years old. Cooking, in general, is one of my favorite things, but making soup is the best thing there is—especially when it's going to a good cause, like Soup Sisters. Giving hearty, delicious soup to those in need is fulfilling, and a feeling I wouldn't trade for anything.

Zac Kara (page 105)

I am 14, live in Orlando, Florida, and was a competitor on the fourth season of *MasterChef Junior*. I love to cook and am always busy trying out new ingredients or techniques. If I am not in the kitchen or playing tennis, then I am working out or playing video games. I also love editing and producing videos for my YouTube channel, youtube.com/c/zackara.

Malcolm Knapp-Durante (page 186)

I am 14 years old and in Grade 9. I absolutely love watching and playing sports of all kinds, especially skiing and golf. I like to support the food bank and I raise funds for them every year by doing a bottle drive. My favorite thing to cook is fig and prosciutto pizza. It's also my favorite thing to eat.

Nicolas Latruwe (page 168)

I am a Grade 7 student at Connect Charter School in Calgary, and I am a soccer player with Calgary Foothills. Cooking and baking are one of my greatest passions, along with soccer. I have been cooking and baking for as long as I can remember. I love the way you can start with such simple ingredients and end up with such complex outcomes.

Lennox Douglas Kane Leaver (page 69)

I am starting Grade 5 French immersion this year and plan to be my nana's translator on a trip to France someday. There we will have *beaucoup fromage pain* and *pain au chocolat*, and sample *soupe de pomme de terre*.

Liam Lewis (page 172)

I am 15 years old. When I'm not busy studying in French, sailing, figure skating, training or eating, I am planning what I'm going to cook or bake next. There are so many great causes I have been involved with, focusing on food and feeding people delicious and healthy meals. I have been very fortunate to have so many awesome food people share their time, skills, recipes and kitchens with me. As much as I can, I would like to repay those people by using my new skills to help others better themselves through food.

Mitchell Loxton (page 133)

I am 12 years old, was born in Bermuda and moved to Canada when I was 3 years old. I now live in Orillia, Ontario. I learned to cook from my mom and my granny, who is a food writer. In addition to cooking, I like to play video games and Lego. I'm interested in space exploration and want to be an aerospace engineer when I grow up.

Abby Major (page 80)

I live in Winchester, Virginia. I am 12 years old and I was a semi-finalist on the TV show *MasterChef Junior*. Besides cooking, I love to read and love animals. I am an avid runner and I also play volleyball.

Julia Mackenzie Martin (page 127)

I am in Grade 6 and love to dance, read and cook. In the kitchen I like to experiment with different and exotic foods. My favorite thing to cook is anything Italian including my own assortment of pasta. Outside the kitchen, I enjoy Girl Guides, the outdoors and camping with my family.

Mario and Klaudia Mihaljevic (page 169)
Mario (9 years old): I love soccer, playing my guitar and accordion and anything to do with trucks, race cars and wildlife. I play the Croatian guitar called the tamburica in the Calgary Croatian Heritage Society. My sister and I are both Earth Rangers and we love to raise money any way we can to save endangered animals. Klaudia (7 years old): I love to sing and dance and anything to do with horses and Monster High. I dance in the young Croatian folklore group in the Calgary Croatian Heritage Society.

Liam Minck (page 177)
I am 11 years old. I like baseball and have my advanced purple belt in martial arts. My job is chopping and slicing in the kitchen with my mom. I like making and eating any soup.

Scott Riege (page 113)
I am 14 years old and I am in Grade 9. I love playing all kinds of sports, especially rugby and badminton. My favorite thing to do is read. If I'm not reading, you'll find me with a friend. What I like most about cooking is that it is a social event; I get to share what I make with family and friends. Someday, I'd like to know how to make a three-course gourmet dinner for my family.

Matthew Sherback (page 63)
I am 12 years old. We had EarthBoxes at my elementary school. Chefs and farmers and other food experts came to visit to talk to us about food and how to cook. One of the visitors was my mom's friend Janice Beaton. My grandma and Janice make cooking fun and taught me about ingredients.

Skylar and Chloe Sinow (page 30)
Skylar (15 years old): I am in Grade 10. I love to cook, garden, mountain bike and ski. I don't have one thing I love to cook the most—I'm all about experimenting and testing new recipes. Chloe (13 years old): I am in Grade 8. I love marketing and business, sewing and fashion design, and am my family's chief recipe taster. I love to bake and am especially fond of making pavlova.

Carson Wiebe (page 166)
I am 12 years old and if I'm not in the kitchen, I will most likely be found at the park playing some of my favorite sports: soccer, tennis and baseball, and hockey in the winter. Aside from main courses, I also like to make desserts and my favorite part of every dish is decorating it. My mom is a major inspiration when I am in the kitchen and she is the one who gave me my interest in cooking.

Jaelie Young (page 118)
I am 9 years old. At home, I like to make supper and bake. I like to bake cookies and cakes. I did some cooking classes at the ATCO Blue Flame Kitchen in Calgary. In my free time I also like to play soccer, basketball and guitar.

Teagan Young (page 57)
I love exploring and being outdoors. When I am outside, you can find me either hiking, biking or camping. I love swimming and am working toward being a lifeguard. When I cook, I like to make salads and experiment with different types of granola protein bars.

my pot runneth over

We are "souper" excited to see our third book come to fruition. Soup Sisters is 8 years old, and the time has gone by very quickly while we continue to grow as an organization that gives so tangibly and from the heart. Meanwhile, our Souper Kids program is also growing steadily, and now this book will be a wonderful addition to our cookbook family.

As always, a new cookbook is a great and lengthy process, and so many people take part in it. My thanks go to all of the chefs, Soup Sisters and Souper Kids from across North America (and even internationally!) that contributed their special recipes and meaningful anecdotes.

I have come to believe that every soup has a story: soup can be a simple gift to family or to strangers, and the giving of soup often creates yet another story in itself. The kids who wrote their stories in the front of the book are proof that soup has meaning to young and older alike! A really "souper" special thanks to all of the kids who contributed recipes with such enthusiasm and authenticity. I hope you'll continue to make soup for others, as I have seen how (rightfully) proud it makes you to offer nourishment and comfort to others.

It's been many years of soup obsession for me, and I thank my family for their generosity in allowing me to fulfill my vision of supporting others in the same way I have supported them. Soup is love, and, of course, a giant "hug in a bowl." Truth be told, I do not have as much time as I would like to make it at home, but my kids, Daniel and Blaire, and my wonderful husband, Garry, simply sit back and let it be as I continue on this epic soup journey.

It was a great pleasure to have the enterprising and inspired energy of Gwendolyn Richards alongside me in the editing, writing and compiling of recipes. Her exuberance jumps off the pages and is perfect for this family edition.

Making the recipes for the photoshoot was no small feat, and I thank all of the amazing volunteers who came out to help us with our soup creations. In turn, Julie Van Rosendaal made them look even more delicious with her magical touch, and the pages of this book are once again graced by her photography and styling, along with support from Sylvia Kong. They both master a special creativity that will have you running to the kitchen with your kids the minute you begin to turn the pages. My heartfelt thanks to both of them for their extreme generosity and enthusiasm for the Soup Sisters organization. Thanks also to The Cookbook Co. for generously providing us their kitchen space for two entire days.

Our brilliant cover photograph was taken once again by the amazing Shallon Cunningham, who volunteered her time only weeks away from having her second child.

Dean Stanton is the creative illustrator extraordinaire! Many years ago he painted my daughter's bedroom furniture, and it has been so fantastic to have his whimsical style back in my world.

The awesome photos from Souper Kids events were contributed by photographers Jennifer Freedman, Andrea Searle, and Jessica Wittman, who volunteer their support all year round.

As always, it is a great pleasure to work with Robert McCullough at Appetite by Random House. Hopefully he has seen me evolve over the years into someone who may actually have a sense of how to create a cookbook. Back in 2012 he had the incredible insight to ask me if I would like to publish a soup cookbook and his instincts, as always, are remarkable. This is sure to be another bestseller and I am eternally grateful for the support of Robert, Lindsay Paterson, and the Appetite team. Elysse Bell and Paige Farrell are both incredible detailists and beyond patient. Elysse has single-handedly coordinated many fast-moving parts; I couldn't have done this without her enduring support and gentle reminders.

I am thankful daily for my assistant Cindi's help with all things soup. She has worked diligently on this cookbook, sending hundreds of emails to our contributors and following up to ensure all the details are in place.

I have had the great privilege of working with Julia Aitken on all three books. She is an extraordinary copyeditor, for whom I am eternally grateful. She makes me look better than I am—what a gift!

Dorothy Sitek of Generation Communications in Vancouver is a longstanding Soup Sisters board member who I can always rely on for a first edit, and to know that she will simply "get" it every time. Thank you my friend, for years of support and mentorship of the highest level.

"Souper" thanks also go to managing editors Susan Traxel, Kimberlee Hesas, and Susan Burns, and designer Rachel Cooper. This book is brilliant because of you!

My most heartfelt thanks to my mother, who raised four kids on fresh and nutritious food even in tough times. From her, we learned that taking care of others through food is high-level love. This early lesson as a child brought me to the belief that maybe I could help make the world a kinder and gentler place with fresh soup made with love.

There are hundreds of volunteers nationwide who I know share that simple belief, and I am thankful every day for each one of you. We are a team of exemplary Soup Sisters and Broth Brothers that are indeed making a difference in the lives of people in crisis. You are the most important ingredients, and together we have provided a recipe for love and comfort to nearly 1 million people whose lives have been affected by family violence. Always soup it forward and deliver to someone in their time of need. We can all do good in the simplest of ways, and providing a "hug in a bowl" has beautiful and long-lasting positive impact for anyone at any time.

metric conversion chart

Weight			Volume	
⅛ oz	4 g		¼ tsp	1 mL
½ oz	15 g		½ tsp	2 mL
1 oz	30 g		1 tsp	5 mL
2 oz	60 g		1 Tbsp	15 mL
3 oz	85 g		1½ Tbsp	22 mL
4 oz/¼ lb	110 g		2 Tbsp	30 mL
5 oz	140 g		3 Tbsp	45 mL
6 oz	170 g		¼ cup	60 mL
7 oz	200 g		⅓ cup	80 mL
8 oz/½ lb	225 g		½ cup	125 mL
9 oz	270 g		⅔ cup	160 mL
12 oz/¾ lb	340 g		¾ cup	185 mL
16 oz/1 lb	450 g		1 cup	250 mL
2 lb	1 kg		1¼ cups	310 mL
3 lb	1.5 kg		1⅓ cups	330 mL
4 lb	1.8 kg		1½ cups	375 mL
5 lb	2.2 kg		**Oven Temperature**	
6 lb	2.7 kg		160°F	70°C
7 lb	3.1 kg		275°F	135°C
8 lb	3.5 g		300°F	150°C
			325°F	160°C
			350°F	175°C
			375°F	190°C
			400°F	200°C
			425°F	220°C
			450°F	230°C

Length			Can and Jar Sizes	
¼ inch	6 mm		7 oz	198 g
½ inch	1.2 cm		8 oz	227 g
¾ inch	2 cm		12 oz	354 mL
1 inch	2.5 cm		14 oz	398 mL
1¼ inches	3 cm		15 oz	425 mL
1½ inches	4 cm		19 oz	540 mL
2 inches	5 cm		24 oz	680 g
3 inches	8 cm		28 oz	796 mL
4 inches	10 cm		48 oz	1.36 L

index